THE SECRET BABBACOMBE MURDER

The mysterious case of John Lee,
"The man they could not hang"

MIKE HOLGATE

Peninsula
Press

ACKNOWLEDGEMENTS

The author extends his sincere thanks to the following people who helped to produce this book:

Wendy Harvey - for assisting with research and typing the original manuscript.

John Pike - for the generous use of his research material and illustrations.

Leslie Lownds Pateman - for access to his pictorial archive of Babbacombe.

Don Collinson, Ray Strevitt, Mike Wells - for interrupting their own research to provide material for this project.

Mark Pool, Lorna Smith, Leslie Byers, Kathy Doust - colleagues at Torquay Reference Library who gave support and helpful advice.

Chris Jackson - for the use of his typewriter and his ability to contact the right people.

Alison and Brian Ainsworth of Peninsula Press for their tireless enthusiasm in putting the book together.

Illustrations

The author and publishers gratefully acknowledge permission granted to reproduce the following illustrations:

John Pike - pp 5, 9, 12, 13, 14 top, 17, 21, 25, 38 top, 43 bottom, 44, 47, 58, 61
Leslie Lownds Pateman - pp 7, 35, 36, 38 bottom, 41, 42 top, 43 top
Devon Library Service - pp 33 top, 34, 42 bottom
Devon & Cornwall Constabulary - pp 3, 10, 14 bottom, 32
Southwark Local Studies Library - p 33 bottom
G A Estate Agents (Torquay) - p 8
Tiverton Museum Society - p 18
Torquay Museum - p 37
The illustrations on pp 4,6 & 23 first appeared in the *Sunday Chronicle* in 1905.
Every effort has been made to trace copyright holders; where this has not been possible, the author and the publishers would be grateful to receive any information in this respect.

Published by Peninsula Press Ltd
P.O. Box 31
Newton Abbot
Devon TQ12 5XH
Tel: 01803 875875

© Mike Holgate 1995

Printed in England by
The Cromwell Press Ltd, Melksham, Wiltshire

ISBN 1 872640 34 6

John Lee - Prisoner L150

CONTENTS

Considering the world-wide fascination with the story of John 'Babbacombe' Lee, and the amount of press coverage the case continues to attract, it is surprising that no book of Lee's life has been published other than his autobiography which first appeared in 1908. There have been privately published booklets, and many authors have devoted a chapter to the subject, though generally, the 'legend' of John Lee has been treated in the same folklore fashion as tales of the Devil on Dartmoor. If the legend of John Lee has proved of more interest than the truth through lack of research, this illustrated history of the life of John Lee proves the adage that truth is often stranger than fiction.

Lee's declaration of innocence from the dock

In the early hours of Saturday 15 November 1884, an elderly spinster Emma Keyse was bludgeoned with an axe and bled to death, her throat slashed with a knife. John Lee, a 20 year old servant at The Glen, Miss Keyse's house, was found guilty of killing his kindly employer. In passing the death sentence, Mr Justice Manisty remarked upon the prisoner's calm demeanour. Speaking for the first time during his trial, Lee answered, 'The reason why I am so calm is that I trust in my Lord and he knows that I am innocent.'

The night before his execution, Lee dreamt he survived three attempts to hang him ...

Eight o'clock on a damp overcast Monday morning, 23 February 1885. An expectant hush fell over the large crowd gathered outside Exeter Prison as the bell tolled. The horrific murder of elderly Emma Keyse at her seaside villa had shocked everyone in the locality. Any moment now they would receive a signal that the perpetrator had paid the penalty for his crime. Minutes later, the on-lookers began to wonder why the black flag

A sketch of Babbacombe Beach in the nineteenth century with The Glen (centre)

had not been raised, perhaps the miserable wretch had finally admitted his guilt and delayed the proceedings by making a protracted confession. Half an hour passed, still no news, it was now thought the condemned man had been granted a last-minute reprieve - maybe there was some truth in the statement he had made to the Vicar of Abbotskerswell, implacating two other people. Speculation continued for a further twenty minutes until, suddenly, members of the press emerged through the prison gate and rushed towards the telegraph office. They were immediately engulfed by people clamouring for information.

A beseiged reporter breathlessly revealed, *'It's a bungle!'*

'What?'

'Can't hang the man!' 'What do you mean?'

'They've tried three times and he's still not dead!'

A thrill of astonishment and disbelief swept through the spectators as the story spread like wild-fire. Special newspaper supplements were on sale two hours later, and the sensational morning's events became the talking point of every town and village in Devon - with the exception of Dartmouth, where the local paper published a somewhat erroneous account of the events:

The condemned man John Lee was executed at Exeter this morning. Berry, who was the executioner gave a seven foot drop. The culprit died easily. The usual inquest was held.

Elsewhere, a remarkable change in public opinion was taking place about the man found guilty of what the trial judge had described, 'one of the most cruel and barbarous murders ever committed.' The man believed to be a villain, capable of the apparently motiveless killing of his kindly employer, began to be the object of some sympathy. Reinforced by the revelation that the prisoner had seen the hanging fail three times in a dream on the eve of the execution, a legend grew up of a poor innocent man they couldn't hang.

——————— PART 1 ———————

CHAPTER 1   PRELUDE TO A TRAGEDY

Emma Ann Keyse

Emma Ann Keyse was born in 1816 at Edmonton, Middlesex, but spent most of her life at The Glen, an idyllic 13 acre estate overlooking the beach, in the South Devon fishing village of Babbacombe. Emma Keyse inherited The Glen upon the death of her mother in 1871, and was charged with selling the house, enabling bequests to be made to other members of the family. Finding a buyer however, proved difficult, but she enjoyed a tranquil unmarried life, accompanied by her faithful servants, Eliza and Jane Neck, who had joined the household in 1836. Emma's two brothers and four sisters from her mother's two marriages all left home to make their own way in the world. Her sisters married men of substance while Emma remained a spinster.

Miss Keyse was considered slightly eccentric and very methodical in her habits. Overtly religious, she attended the parish church of St Marychurch and conducted morning and evening prayers with her servants. She stayed up late making religious notes in her diary and often ventured out on to the verandah in the early hours of the morning to hear the church clock striking. She was renowned for her kindness.

In 1878, she needed a boy to care for an elderly pony and carry out odd jobs. Her young cook, Millie suggested that her brother could fill the post and arranged an interview for the youngster who was offered the job - his name was John Lee.

JOHN LEE

The Lee family lived in Abbotskerswell, a small Devon village of some 450 people, situated 1 1/2 miles south of Newton Abbot and 6 miles north-east of Torquay.

John Henry George Lee was born at 1 Elm Cottage, on 15 August 1864, the second child of John and Mary, and attended the village school with his sister Amelia who was two years older. The children also had a half-sister, Elizabeth Harris, the illegitimate daughter of their mother, who lived with her grandparents in the nearby village of Kingsteignton. All three children, known to the family as Jack, Millie, and Lizzie, would at some point find employment in the service of Emma Keyse, owner of The Glen on Babbacombe Beach.

John's father was a clay-miner and also farmed a small piece of land, while his widowed grandfather, who lived with the family, was a boot-maker. By Victorian standards, the family was well provided for.

At about the age of 14, John left the village to join his sister working in the gracious surroundings of The Glen. Within a few months the young man had developed a passion for the sea. His favourite pastime was to sit on Babbacombe Beach listening to the tales of the old sailors, while admiring the vessels which frequented the Bay. Against strong opposition from his parents, he left The Glen on 1 October 1879 to join the Royal Navy.

NAVAL RATING LEE - SERVICE NO. 110179

Away I went with all my papers in order. After saying good-bye to my father and mother I left for Newton Abbot, and thence went to the depot at Exeter. At Exeter I met a lot of other boys who had been drafted down from London. In a few days we found ourselves on board the Circe at Plymouth and I was on the way to being a sailor in Her Majesty's Navy.

From the Circe I went to H.M.S. Implacable, where I remained till I was a first-class boy. When I left the Implacable I carried away with me a prize which is on the table before me now. It is called "The Bear Hunters of the Rocky Mountains" by Anne Bowman. On the fly-leaf is the following inscription:-

H.M.S. IMPLACABLE, Xmas,1880
Admiralty Prize for general progress First prize, first instruction.
Awarded to John Lee.
(Signed) B. Jackson, Commander.

I had found a profession. I was doing well.

Next, I joined the training brig Liberty, and was afterwards sent to the Foudroyant for gunnery training. I was now eighteen. In a few months I would have been rated as an ordinary seaman, when a misfortune befell me that was to be the first of a long series of troubles. I was stricken down with pneumonia, and sent to the Royal Naval Hospital. For some days I lay between life and death till they pulled me through - but at what a price! The doctors told me that I was no more use to the Navy. I was invalided out. My career was closed. I still possess my discharge paper, setting forth the reason of my discharge and describing my character as 'Very good'. My heart was broken. There seemed to be nothing left for me to do. (From Lee's autobiography)

HOMEWARD BOUND

Dicharged from the Navy on 6 January 1882 on medical grounds, John returned to South Devon and obtained employment in Kingswear as 'boots' at the Yacht Club Hotel, later named the Royal Dart Hotel. Dissatisfied with this job he became a porter on Kingswear Railway Station and a month later, on 9 October, he was transferred to the goods department at Torre Station, Torquay. He had only been there a week before Emma Keyse used her influence to

Ridgehill today, now called Taplow Court

find him a position as footman to Colonel Brownlow at his Torquay residence, Ridgehill, situated in the Warberries.

Six months later Lee was arrested in Plymouth attempting to pawn the Brownlow family silver. He later claimed he stole the items to raise money for a friend who was emigrating to Australia, but offered no defence at his trial. He pleaded guilty to having stolen the property of his master on 28 April 1883 and was sentenced to six months' hard labour at Exeter Assizes in July. Emma Keyse came to his aid once more when she wrote to the Chaplin of Exeter Prison, the Reverend Pitkin on New Year's Day 1884.

I hope you will excuse my troubling you, but I feel anxious to know what report you can give me of John Lee. Whether he has conducted himself satisfactorily, and whether those who have had much to do with him can give a good report, and whether you consider that he truly and really feels the great sin he has been led into, and whether he is really penitent. I shall be grateful if you will make careful enquiries, in addition to your own personal opinion. He lived with me as a lad, and I liked him very much, and found him very honest and truthful and obedient. I had no particular fault to find with him, but considered his was a simple-minded, easy disposition that would be easily led astray, and hoped, by being on a training ship, he would gain stability of character and purpose, and was very sorry that his health would not admit of his remaining. I feel much interested in his family and himself: and I have told his mother that I will take him back into my service, and to work in the garden with my gardener for a while, to be able to give him a character, until something desirable may turn up.

RETURN TO THE GLEN

John Lee gratefully accepted Miss Keyse's offer to return to The Glen, where his half-sister, Elizabeth Harris had replaced his sister Millie as cook.

At first, all went well, and he became engaged to a twenty-year-old local dressmaker. Kate Farmer lived at 3 Grafton Terrace, Ellacombe, with her young brother Ernest, and their mother Harriet, who died suddenly aged forty-nine. A few days after accompanying his fianceé to the funeral, Lee added to her grief. He had become despondent about his future prospects and did not feel he could contemplate marriage until his situation improved. He wrote to Kate on 10 October, suggesting that they call off their relationship, as he was unsettled and planned to 'leave the town as soon as possible'. Miss Farmer, clearly shocked and distressed, changed his mind with the following reply:

Kate Farmer, Lee's fiancée

As you are so undecided about what you intend to do with the future, are you also undecided about me? Do you think seriously of what you are doing before you give me up, I tell you now the same as I told you before, our engagement shall not be broken off with my consent. As regards what you intend in the future, if it was to be your lot to break stones in the street. I will not say no. Have a little pity for me and think how dearly I love you.

A NEW OWNER FOR THE GLEN

Babbacombe Beach (circa 1875) with The Glen (right)

John Lee's engagement to Kate Farmer soon made him dissatisfied with life at The Glen. He felt that he was working for a token allowance in an effort to redeem his character, and that Miss Keyse was not doing enough to find him a more lucrative position that would enable him to marry.

Repeated applications had in fact been made on his behalf, but with the experience of Colonel Brownlow fresh in the minds of prospective employers, even a lady of Emma Keyse's influence could not persuade anyone to 'give the poor boy a chance'.

Further reason for Lee's anxiety was the impending London auction of The Glen, for his services would then no longer be required. Matters came to a head on 28 October when the estate was sold for £13,000. That evening Lee had a furious row with his employer and she reduced his miserly wage from 2s 6d to 2s a week. He stormed into the kitchen in tears and told his half-sister, Elizabeth Harris, that he would not stay a moment longer and would have his revenge. Next morning he met the village postman, William Richards, and told him that Miss Keyse had begged him to stay as there was a possibility that the new owner would keep him on.

The tragic events that were about to occur meant that the purchase would fall through, and when the property was put up for auction again, it failed to raise a bid of £2,000. The Reverend Wrey of St Marychurch summed up the change in attitude to The Glen in an emotional sermon:

This unique spot on earth, favoured so lavishly by Nature, favoured by Royalty and every other visitor, will henceforth be marked and known - oh, horrors! - thus, 'See that yonder glen and that thatched house by the seaside? That is the scene of that atrocious and vile murder of 1884.'

CHAPTER 2 THE NIGHT IN QUESTION

The small village of Babbacombe, about one and a half miles from Torquay, was thrown into a state of the wildest excitement on Saturday morning by a report that an aged and well-known lady of the place had been cruelly and brutally murdered. At first the rumours were believed to be exaggerated, but as the morning wore on, and more details came to light, the conviction gained ground that a terrible deed had been committed - mysteriously, silently, and with a fiendish disregard of other lives in the house, and of the premises, and their handsome contents - for all appearances point to the conclusion that the hand which did the murder, if murder it be, set fire to the house, with the intention, undoubtedly, of hiding all traces of the ghastly act.

(Torquay Times 21 Nov 1884)

The body of Emma Keyse was found by her servants in the early hours of Saturday morning, 15 November, 1884. She had suffered a broken skull, a cut throat, her body had been set alight and an attempt had been made to burn the house down.

The police started piecing together the events of the evening. At 5.30 pm Elizabeth Harris, who was expecting a child, had gone to bed feeling unwell. John Lee went out at 7 pm to post letters, then met his fiancée, Kate Farmer, returning to The Glen shortly after 10 pm. Evening prayers were conducted by Miss Keyse before Lee went to bed at 11 pm.

The Neck sisters, Eliza and Jane, carried out their duties, locking doors and windows, before making tea and toast for themselves, and preparing some cocoa for Miss Keyse which they left on the stove. Eliza and Jane retired to bed at 12.40 am after handing the house keys to their mistress who was writing in her diary in the dining-room.

It seemed that Miss Keyes had taken the cocoa to her room and had partially changed into her night attire. Whether she heard a disturbance and discovered an arsonist, or the house was set on fire later to disguise a greater crime is not clear, but for some reason, she descended the stairs and met her death in the hall. Her body was then dragged into the dining-room and set on fire.

At some time between 3 and 4 am, Elizabeth Harris smelt smoke and aroused the Neck sisters. Help was summoned and the blaze brought under control. John Lee was sent to the village of Compton to inform Miss Keyse's half-sister of the tragedy. When he returned, the police had formed their conclusions.

After receiving medical attention for cuts on his arm, Lee was informed by the police at 10 am that he was to be placed under arrest on suspicion of murder. In reply to the charge he appeared shaken, but answered simply, 'Oh on suspicion. That's all right.'

Jane Neck, parlourmaid

Eliza Neck, Lady's maid

John Lee, general servant

Elizabeth Harris, cook

THE HOUSEHOLD STAFF

On the fateful night, the Neck sisters were awoken by the cries of Elizabeth Harris who had seen smoke coming into her room. Eliza Neck went downstairs and saw John Lee, fully dressed, at the foot of the stairs. Going into the dining-room, she found the body of Miss Keyse and the whole room smouldering.

Ignoring Eliza's pleas to seek help from their nearest neighbour at the Cary Arms Inn, Lee helped Jane Neck to descend the stairs by putting his arm around her waist and taking hold of her arm. When the nightgown was examined later, marks of blood were found on the sleeve where he had placed his hand.

Jane opened the dining-room shutters and windows, then stepped out on to the lawn and called for help. Receiving no response, she returned to the room and implored Lee to fetch assistance. Later, after help had arrived, she noticed broken glass on the dining-room carpet and saw Lee outside. On the spot where he was standing were fresh spots of blood. The manservant claimed he had cut his arm by breaking a window from inside the house to let out the smoke, but the glass had clearly been smashed from outside.

The weight of circumstantial evidence and the testimony of the female servants led the police to one conclusion, Lee was the culprit. Later, writing from prison to his sister Millie, Lee complained bitterly, 'They have not told six words of truth, that is, the servants and that lovely step-sister, who carries her character with her.'

Part of the illustrated newspaper supplement on the crime

THE SCENE OF THE CRIME

The *Devon County Standard* newspaper issued an illustrated supplement which showed how the elderly victim was struck down in the hall after descending the stairs, less than six feet from the pantry where John Lee slept. The body was then dragged into the dining-room and set alight using oil kept in a cupboard behind Lee's fold-up bed; other fires were started in various parts of the house.

The blood-stained knife identified as the murder weapon was usually kept on the hall table but was found in a drawer in the pantry; a hatchet used in the attack, normally kept in the garden shed, was produced immediately by Lee to fight the fire when the alarm was given.

Neighbours summoned to help control the fire at The Glen, including local fishermen and officers from the coastguard station, estimated that the fire in the bedroom had been started only a few minutes before their arrival, while the blaze in the dining-room had been smouldering for over an hour before taking a hold. The Fire Service was unable to descend the steep cliff path to the beach to render assistance, but the flames were quickly brought under control. The first person on the scene, landlord of the Cary Arms, William Gasking, conceded how close the murderer had come to destroying all traces of the crime:

William Gasking, one of the first on the scene

I said to Lee 'What's the matter, John?' and he replied 'Missis is burnt to death.' There was a lot of smoke coming from the dining-room and I went in there. It was as much as I could do to get in, the smoke was so stifling. When I was inside I saw Miss Keyse on the floor. I put one arm under her head and the other under the lower part of her body, and called to John to do the same. After we had taken the body out we went back and, with the aid of some coastguardmen, extinguished the fire. If we had been ten minutes later it would have been a hopeless job.

THE ARREST

Police Sergeant Abraham Nott who carried out the preliminary investigation at The Glen was also the man who arrested Lee.

Nott was later to be praised by the coroner for his meticulous presentation of the evidence accumulated at the scene of the crime and the jury - all either friends or acquaintances of the victim - presented their expenses to police funds in recognition of his work. Lee described his arrest in his autobiography:

Immediately after I had been arrested I was marched all the way to Torquay police-station in front of a policeman.

Police Sergeant Abraham Nott

No crowd accompanied me. I was not handcuffed. I simply trudged along as if I was bent on some errand. Behind me was the sergeant. I made no attempt to escape. I wanted to se the whole business through from beginning to end. I had nothing to be afraid of. In a sense I was quite happy.

When we got to Torquay I was formally charged, and put into a cell. As I heard the door clang upon me my heart sank. For a second time I was within prison walls. I sat down, my head in my hands, and strove to realise what had befallen me. Theft I had suffered for. I was now charged with murder!

The Chief Constable of Devon, Captain de Courcy Hamilton was a close friend of Emma Keyse and took personal charge of the investigation into her death. He was eager to prove that the local force could bring the case to a successful conclusion without interference from Scotland Yard who sent a detective to conduct an independent enquiry.

Captain de Courcy Hamilton

CHAPTER 3 THE SCALES OF JUSTICE

The Coroner, S.Hacker Esq.

The first chapter, and the second, in the story of the Babbacombe Tragedy has been brought to a close this week. The Coroner's Inquest has resulted in a verdict of wilful murder against John Lee, who was taken into custody on the morning of Miss Keyse's death, and the Magistrates have committed him for trial at the next Assizes on the charge of murder and arson.
(*Torquay Times*, 5 Dec 1884)

John Lee was greatly disadvantaged at the outset of the legal proceedings as he was unrepresented in court, much to the concern of many observers including the correspondent of the *Western Morning News:*

It is high time that John Lee was provided with professional assistance. When a young and comparatively uninstructed man is charged with a crime of the greatest possible enormity, it is a dangerous thing for him to try to cross-examine witnesses. In such a case, he needs legal advice - if only to tell him to hold his tongue.

Solicitor R Gwynne Templer came to Lee's aid and the prisoner reserved his defence. The trial was set to take place before Mr Justice Manisty at Exeter Castle commencing Monday 2 February 1885.

Preparations for Lee's defence however, were seriously disrupted when Gwynne Templer was suddenly taken ill and replaced by his 22 year-old-brother. Lee was only informed of the change two days before his trial when Charles Templer visited him in prison to discuss the case.

'Shall I have anything to say, sir?' enquired Lee.

'No,' replied the young solicitor, 'Don't you say a word, I'll get you off all right.'

The Babbacombe Murder was featured on the cover of the *Illustrated Police News* and was given prominent coverage in the national press which brought the following comment in an editorial of the *Torquay Times:*

Horror at the tragic fate of a highly respected lady whose long life had been spent in this neighbourhood has been the prevailing sensation during the last week. Babbacombe, the name of a delightful marine village, well known to residents and visitors in Torquay but very little known by others, has suddenly attained an

The Babbacombe murder made the national Illustrated Police News three weeks later

unenviable notoriety and become a household word all over the country . . . The mystery which therefore still enshrouds the fearful crime stimulates the public curiosity, while the shocking details are horrible enough to satisfy the most morbid craving for sensation. We hope that before many days have passed the painful enquiry may be completed and the mystery solved so that the public mind may not be kept long in a state of such painful uncertainty as exists at present; and that the responsibility for the terrible crime may be brought clearly home to the true culprit; and then fiat justitia!

Lines on the Committal of John Lee for the murder of Miss Keyse

This lyric about the Babbacombe Murder was sung to a popular tune of the day called 'Driven from Home' and appeared on a broadsheet published in Bristol after the Magistrates' Hearing.

In Babbacombe village not long ago,
An old maiden lady has met her death blow,
So cruelly murdered and then set on fire,
By the hands of a villain that was his desire,
Her throat was cut in a most barbarous way,
The poor lifeless body in the dining-room lay,
They aroused the neighbours, but it was too late,
Miss Keyse had met with this terrible fate.

John Lee, the Butler, is now sent for trial,
Committed for murder there is no denial,
Whether he did it, it is hard to say,
It will be proved on some future day,

John Lee is but twenty years old,
He bears a bad name so we are told,
By the judge he will soon have to stand,
To be tried for murder in his own native land,
If he is guilty the jury will say,
And then on the gallows the penalty he will pay,
Such a crime was seldom heard of before,
It is a disgrace to our native shore,

Miss Keyse's body now lies in the grave,
In the silent grave where wild flowers wave,
Her soul gone to rest with the angels on high,
In a brighter land far beyond the blue sky,
Her neighbours they miss her both rich and poor,
Beloved by all along the sea shore,
Nearly seventy years she had spent in this world,
But now she has been to Eternity hurled,

The old lady spoke to her butler one day,
And advised him to emigrate far away,
Her wages being so very small,
She did not care to keep him at all,
John Lee said to his half-sister one day,
He would burn the house down in a mysterious way,
It looks very black against him so we are told,
The house set on fire and her body was cold,

When charged with the murder he had nothing to say,
Some things have been found that he threw away,
The axe has been analysed and blood has been found,
With it the victim was struck to the ground,
Her body was covered all over with gore,
In her nightdress she lay on the floor,
The murder is one of the worst ever known,
To be burnt and destroyed in her quiet little home,

Miss Keyse lived in retirement not far from Torquay,
In a quiet little spot facing the sea,
Her friends and relations now will deplore,
Although she has gone to that brighter shore,
They have laid her so tenderly down to her rest,
Beautiful flowers now cover her breast,
Miss Keyse in Heaven with angels will dwell,
Far from the place where by murder she fell.

HANG THE TRUTH - PRINT THE LIE!

The Babbacombe Murder became international news when the following highly imaginative and colourful account of the murder of 'Miss Key' (*sic*) was telegraphed across the Atlantic and appeared in the *New York Herald* and the *Toronto Globe* setting the tone for the way the story has been covered for over a century. The newspaper editor's dictum,' If the legend is more interesting than the truth, print the legend', certainly applies to the case of John Lee.

Torquay, the fashionable winter watering place on the south coast, is at present stirred by a sensation of a most ghastly character. Nearly adjoining Torquay is the smart fishing village of Babbacombe. Conspicuous for many years among the residents of Babbacombe has been Miss Key an aristocratic, wealthy and unmarried woman of middle age. The lady resided in a palatial villa and was regarded by the families of the fishermen as an angel because of charities, and her accomplishments and entertainments were the envy of most of the fashionable visitors to Torquay. Some time ago Miss Key took into her personal service, as a valet, a young and good-looking man, named John Lee. He had come down from London, and bore such testimonials as to worth and character from personal friends of the Key family that he found little difficulty in entering the service of the lady. His duties finally resolved themselves into those of an escort, and he waited upon his patron wherever she went. This started much gossip on the part of the envious, and this gossip gradually became quite exaggerated. Last night the people of Babbacombe were startled by the discovery of flames issuing from the mansion in which Miss Key resided. The fire had evidently been burning for some time, as the flames broke simultaneously through windows in the different walls. The villagers went to the scene in a body and the coast guard and local police soon got control of the fire from without. They found that the mansion had been securely closed and that the windows and doors had all been fastened. An entrance was forced and the fire extinguished. Miss Key was found lying upon the parlour floor - dead. Her person was nude, and the body partly charred. An investigation revealed the fact that her throat had been cut and her skull fractured.

There were evidences that the lady had been dragged down stairs before she was killed, and that preceding all this and after a terrible struggle in her private apartments she had been assaulted. All the jewellery and portable valuables belonging to the lady were missing, and not a shilling of money was left in the house. The murder was at once set down to jealousy, and the robbery was set down as a ruse to misdirect suspicion. No trace of John Lee could be found, and it was feared that he too had been murdered. The country was at once scoured by the police and the enraged fishermen who eagerly joined in the chase for the criminals. After an all-night search John Lee was found concealed in a stable not far from the scene of the murder. A large sum of money and much of the missing jewellery were found upon his person. He was at once arrested and charged with the crime.

He confessed his guilt and fully told the story. He admitted he was an ex-convict and had obtained employment in the service of Miss Key, by means of forged letters. He said he had fallen in love with the lady, and having no means to secure an acquaintance with her, resorted to his deceit for that purpose. After he had been in her employ for a time and had secured kindly recognition in his capacity as valet, his ardour getting the better of his judgment; he mistook the lady's favours for more than it meant, and made an avowal of love.

Miss Key was horrified, and attempted to correct his folly by showing him that his suit was both hopeless and absurd. He persisted, and Miss Key finally ordered him out of her service and accused him of being a mercenary adventurer. On the evening of the murder he forced another interview upon his mistress, and when she again treated his overtures with contempt he became enraged and attacked her.

His passions once aroused he lost all control of his moral senses he said, and after the assault he struck her senseless so that she could not interfere with his escape. When he saw that the blow was apparently fatal, he resolved to rob the house and flee. After he had gathered up his plunder he noticed signs of consciousness in his victim, and then being desperate broke her skull and cut her throat. It then occurred to him, to drag the remains down stairs, close the doors and windows and fire the house in the hope of burying the crime in mystery. He believed that if he could have got out of the country, the crime would never have been attributed to him. The prisoner is under special guard, threats of mob violence having been made against him.

THE CASE FOR THE PROSECUTION

The case for the Crown was presented by two eminent counsels, Mr A Collins QC and Mr Vigor, instructed by Torquay solicitor Isidore Carter. The evidence against Lee was circumstantial but considerable, and 26 witnesses were called upon to give evidence. The main points of the prosecution's case were as follows.

* The victim was murdered in the hall only five foot nine inches from the entrance to the pantry where Lee slept in a fold-down bed.

* Lee claimed he was asleep and heard nothing, even though the partition dividing the pantry from the hall did not reach the ceiling. The door of the pantry was always left open and the fire in the hall could be seen from Lee's bed. Smoke from the fire would have overcome a sleeping person.

* A knife usually kept on the hall table was found in a drawer in the pantry. It was stained with blood and some paper found nearby looked as if it had been used to wipe the blade.

* The body and various parts of the house had been set alight using oil from a can kept in a cupboard beside Lee's bed. The cork from the blood-stained oil-can was found on the floor of the pantry.

* To take the oil-can from the cupboard and replace it after use, the murderer would have had to pass through a 2 ¹/₂" gap between the end of the bed and the wall without disturbing Lee.

* Dr Steele who examined the dead woman, found that a blood-stained hatchet matched the wound in the victim's head. The hatchet was usually kept in an outhouse but was produced immediately by Lee to help the fire-fighters cut away burning timbers.

* Government analyst Dr Stephenson examined the prisoner's clothes and noticed that an attempt had been made to wash off spots of blood. The clothes also smelt strongly of oil, and hair on Lee's socks corresponded with that of the victim.

* Matches found on the floor in Miss Keyse's bedroom were a similiar type to those dicovered in Lee's trouser pocket.

* Panes of glass in the dining-room had been broken by Lee who claimed he did it to allow the smoke to escape, but the windows had clearly been smashed from the outside, evidently - claimed the prosecution - to self-inflict wounds on his arm and provide an alibi for the blood on his clothes.

* When the alarm was raised, Lee helped Jane Neck down the stairs. There were marks of blood on her night-dress where he had put his arm around her.

* Lee had made threats against Miss Keyse in conversations with the village postman.

* Elizabeth Harris revealed that her half-brother had threatened to set fire to the house and watch it burn from the top of the hill, if his employer would not give him a reference when he left. On another occasion when Miss Keyse had criticised his work, he said he would like to throw her over a cliff.

* There were no signs of a forced entry and nothing had been stolen. Therefore, it was contended, the murder must have been committed by a member of the household. John Lee was the only servant with a grievance against his employer, having had his wages reduced, and the only person physically capable of inflicting such injuries on the victim.

William Richards, postman: Lee told me, 'I've got tired of this place and if Miss Keyse don't get me a place soon, she will soon wish she had or I will put a end to one before I leave.'

Dr William Stott Steele, physician: '... the square-shaped depression in the skull is a little larger than the head of the hatchet itself, but compares exactly with it.'

Elizabeth Harris, half-sister: John said, 'If she won't give me a character I'll level the place to ashes.'

THE CASE FOR THE DEFENCE

John Lee was represented by Mr W Molesworth St Aubyn, Member of Parliament for Helston in Cornwall, who had earlier prosecuted Lee when he was convicted of theft.

Court procedures at the time did not allow prisoners to speak in their own defence and, with the enforced absence of R Gwynne Templer, Lee's representatives were poorly prepared. Sergeant Knott spent two and a half hours on the witness stand giving evidence for the prosecution but was not cross examined. No witnesses were called on Lee's behalf, and the defence amounted to no more than a general submission that the evidence was circumstantial and failed to prove the prosecution's case. In particular, it did not make the most of the following points.

* Lee was sent to Compton to inform the victim's relatives of the tragedy. He had every opportunity to make his escape, yet he returned. Was this the act of a guilty man?

*Emma Keyse had been Lee's benefactor and after her murder he told PC Boughton, 'I have lost my best friend'.

*It was claimed that Lee was a heavy sleeper. The servants often worked in the pantry without waking him. He said he did not hear anything until woken by the shouts of the servants. Eliza Neck admitted that it was possible to squeeze past the bottom of Lee's bed to reach the cupboard where the oil was kept.

*Traces of blood, oil and hair found on Lee's clothing occurred when he helped to carry the corpse out of the dining room.

*Blood marks found on Jane Neck's dress came from a cut on Lee's arm caused, he said when he put his fist through a window to let out smoke from the house-fire.

* The police stated that there was no sign of a forced entry, but an intruder would have been able to gain entry by other means. Jane Neck testified that she did not lock one of the French windows as Miss Keyse often walked onto the verandah late at night before retiring.

* The prosecution suggested that the murder was premeditated, as the hatchet said to have been used to strike the victim was usually kept in an outhouse. This being the case, why did the attack not take place while Miss Keyse was writing in her diary in the dining-room, or in her bedroom after allowing time for her to fall asleep? What led her to descend the stairs after preparing for bed?

*Dr Chilcote did not agree with Dr Steele that the hatchet had caused the head wounds and agreed only with the greatest reluctance that the small knife produced by the prosecution could have inflicted the throat wound which was a deep cut through to the vertebrae.

*Threats against Miss Keyse were admitted but defence counsel submitted that anyone who seriously intended to carry out such an attack would not speak to others about it.

*Elizabeth Harris was expecting a child and her lover could have been concealed in the house on the night of the murder. The defence did not attempt to elicit the name of her lover, but proposed that he may have committed the murder then put the knife in the pantry to throw suspicion on Lee. It was not suggested that Harris herself was involved with the crime, but she might be screening her lover by testifying against Lee.

* In his summing up, defence counsel asked the Jury to disregard any prejudicial comments they may have heard or read outside the court. (One example of this concerned newspaper comments to the effect that Lee was upset at being excluded from Miss Keyse's Will. Her Will had in fact been made in 1875, therefore Lee could not have felt any grievance about being denied a bequest.)

THE SUMMING UP

The trial reached its conclusion on the third day and the verdict was reported in *The Times:*

Mr Justice Manisty

The Learned Judge, in summing up, said that the case had been justly described as one of circumstantial evidence, but the jury must bear in mind that that class of evidence was occasionally more conclusive than direct evidence. . .

It was certain that the motive for this murder was not plunder, but the almost dark insinuation by the learned counsel for the defence that the murder might have been committed by a third person because Elizabeth Harris had a lover was very far-fetched indeed. If the evidence for the prosecution was to be believed, it was clear that the statement of the prisoner that Lee was sound asleep at the time of the alarm and required to be aroused was untrue. With regard to the threats which had been uttered, it was urged on the one side that these threats were indicative of vengeful intention, and, on the other, that if the prisoner had really entertained any such intention he would certainly have preserved silence. The matter was one entirely for their consideration, and in this, as in all other parts of the case, they would doubtless give full weight to every argument in favour of the prisoner.

The case was not only one of deliberate murder, but of a deliberate and prolonged attempt to conceal the crime after it was committed. It was for them to consider whether this murder could have been committed without the prisoner having the slightest notion of what was going on, or that the house could have been set on fire in five distinct places without his hearing any movement or noticing any smell of fire. They must approach the case with an assumption in favour of the innocence of the prisoner, and, whatever might be the result, he had never met a case where the evidence had been more fairly given, or its conduct had been more efficient.

VERDICT AND SENTENCE

The jury retired to consider their verdict, and, after an absence of nearly 40 minutes, returned, saying they found the prisoner guilty.

In answer to the usual question why judgment should not be passed upon him, the prisoner said he was innocent.

His lordship, in passing sentence, said the prisoner had been found guilty, on the clearest evidence, of one of the most cruel and barbarous murders that had ever been committed. Throughout the trial the prisoner had maintained a calm and collected demeanour, which had not even left him at that fearful moment; but such behaviour was not impossible to a man who could commit so terrible a crime. After passing formal sentence of death, and warning the prisoner that he could not hope for any mercy, the learned judge exhorted him to spend his few remaining days on earth in preparation for the next world.

The prisoner, before being removed from the dock, said, 'The reason, my lord, why I am so calm and collected is because I trust in my Lord, and He knows I am innocent.'

Following Lee's arrest, The *Torquay Times* reported: 'It is said that the young fellow in custody has of late manifested signs of not being quite right in the mind.' It went on to comment, 'There is a peculiarity about the eyes; they lack lustre and expression, and are such as may be met with in our lunatic asylums.' Lee's parents also revealed that he had often acted in the past 'as though he was not right'. This view echoed that of many observers of Lee's demeanour in court:

The behaviour of the prisoner all through the case has been one of supreme indifference; indeed, at times, he has recognised his acquaintances in Court and winked and nodded in a manner as if the charge against him was one of the most trivial character instead of being one which imperilled his life.

(Torquay Directory)

The foreman of the jury expressed the opinion that, had the defendant pleaded insanity, the verdict returned would have been very different.

As a last resort, a petition was organised by the Vicar of Abbotskerswell asking the Home Secretary to reprieve Lee on the grounds of his youth and an unsound mind. This was unsuccessful.

Lee's mother went to see her son for the last time before the appointed execution and found him to be totally unconcerned about his fate, cheerful, and behaving, she said, 'as if he were going to a theatre'.

CHAPTER 4 A BUNGLE ON THE SCAFFOLD

THE BABBICOMBE MURDER- SHOCKING SCENES ON THE SCAFFOLD

Illustrated Police News

Anxious officials assembled nervously on the scaffold. It was their painful duty to witness the execution of John Lee, and more than one had fortified himself with a drop of courage, though nothing could have prepared them for the harrowing scenes that were to follow. The executioner, James Berry, quickly pinioned the condemned man, drew a white cap over his head, then tightened the noose around his neck.

'Have you anything to say?' he whispered.

'No', came the firm reply, 'Drop away'!

The hangman hesitated while the Prison Chaplin concluded the service from the Burial of the Dead:

'Now is the Christ risen from the dead . . .'

At the appropriate moment, Berry pulled a lever to activate the 'drop', then gasped in amazement as the trap-door merely sagged two inches, leaving the prisoner precariously suspended between life and death!

'Quick stamp on it'! he shouted to the warders.

Distressing scenes followed as desperate efforts were made to force the trap open. Warders virtually jumped on the doors and risked falling into the pit with the prisoner had they been successful, but after several minutes, the bewildered prisoner was led to one side, while the apparatus was tested and found to work perfectly. Visibly shaken, Berry made a second attempt, but to no avail. Heaving with all his might, he succeeded only in bending the lever.

'This is terrible,' cried the anguished Governor.

'Take the prisoner away!'

An artisan warder was summoned to diagnose the problem and a saw passed around the frame of the trap-door to relieve possible pressure on the wooden boards, swollen by overnight rain.

Satisfied that the fault had now been remedied, the Governor recalled the prisoner to face his ordeal for a third time. The witnesses were in a great state of shock and the Chaplain trembled as he read a passage from the service

'The last enemy to be destroyed is death.'

Perspiring freely, Berry grasped the lever with both hands, determined that this time, John Lee would keep his appointment in Hell! The bolt was drawn and the scaffold shuddered.

'Is it all over?' pleaded the Chaplain, afraid to look.

'In God's name, put a stop to this!' exclaimed Mr Caird, the surgeon.

The Reverend Pitkin opened his eyes and almost collapsed when he realised that Lee had survived a third attempt on his life. He immediately informed the Under-Sherrif, Mr H James,

'I cannot carry on!'

Without the presence of a Chaplin to sign the death certificate, the execution could not continue, therefore it was agreed to postpone the proceedings pending instructions from the Home Secretary.

John Lee was returned to his cell, seemingly unaffected by his torment, but reacted angrily when Berry came in to remove his bonds.

'Don't do that', he protested, 'I want to be hung!'

'Have no fear,' reassured the Chaplain, with tears in his eyes,

'By the laws of England they cannot put you on the scaffold again!'

Lee recovered his composure, then suddenly remembered an extraordinary occurrence which he recounted to the incredulous Chaplain:

'I saw it all in a dream! I was led down to the scaffold and it would not work - after three attempts, they brought me back to my cell!'

The Reverend Pitkin's assurance to Lee that he was legally protected from having to face the death penalty again was misinformed. However, the Home Secretary, Sir William Harcourt, was enpowered to commute the sentence on humanitarian grounds if he felt it appropriate.

Lee's agonising experience brought about a wave of public sympathy and indignation typified by Queen Victoria who reacted strongly in favour of Lee, even though she had been personally acquainted with the murder victim. She made her feelings known in a telegram to the Home Secretary:

> *'I am horrified at the disgraceful scenes at Exeter at Lee's execution. Surely Lee cannot now be executed. It would be too cruel. Imprisonment for life seems the only alternative.*

Sir William concurred and told a packed House of Commons,

> *'It would shock the feelings of everyone if a man had twice to pay the pangs of imminent death.'*

Mr St Aubyn, who had conducted the inept defence of Lee could not disguise his relief in a letter to the Reverend Pitkin:

> *'I am one of those who was never satisfied of his guilt. What a marvellous thing if he turns out to be innocent. At any rate he must have a nerve of iron. What will become of him now, I wonder?'*

PRISONER NO. L 150

Following Lee's amazing escape from the death penalty, the Home Secretary ordered that he be held at 'her Majesty's pleasure', with a recommendation that he should never be released.

Leaving Exeter Prison in March 1885, Lee spent brief periods in solitary confinement at Pentonville and Wormwood Scrubs before being transferred to Portsmouth Prison on 28 October, 1885. In 1892, he made a final move to Portland Prison where he served the remainder of a sentence he later described as a 'living death'.

In 1905, the Home Secretary resisted increasing pressure to review the case. *The Daily Mail's* Parliamentary Correspondent agreed saying:

> *People forget that the case of Lee is altogether different from those of other murderers. Lee was not reprieved because the merits of his case justified the step, but because of the miserable bungle which was made in attempting to hang him.*

MPs took up Lee's case and at one point rumours of his imminent release resulted in a huge crowd assembling at Weymouth Railway Station, hoping to catch a glimpse of Lee arriving from Portland. *The Sunday Chronicle* serialised Lee's story and published letters written by the prisoner declaring his innocence and urging readers to petition the Secretary of State on his behalf. Further pressure was exerted on the authorities by Lee who sought permission to improve his appearance before his discharge. He had a set of false teeth fitted and was allowed to grow his hair. A former inmate of Portland Prison talked to *Lloyd's Weekly News* about Lee's plans for the future:

> *'He expects to make a vast sum of money by giving lectures and by the sale of his book. He speaks as if he has some tremendous revelations to make. . .'*

CHAPTER 5 FREE AT LAST

At eight o'clock on the morning of the 18 December 1907 the iron gates of a prison opened, and out into the light of day stepped two middle-aged men. One of them was an official in civilian clothes. He bore the hallmarks of drill and discipline. The other man ... The other man. There was something strange about him. He looked hunted and cowed, like a creature crushed and broken. He seemed to hang back as if he were afraid of the light of day. He appeared to draw no happy inspiration from God's sunshine. He fumbled at his overcoat pockets as if the very possession of a pocket was a new sensation. He trod gingerly, as if the earth concealed a gaping hole. Away they went

John Lee is welcomed home by the Reverend Gordon Campbell of Abbotskerswell

by cab and rail to Newton Abbot. There the two men walked to the police station, where the official announced that he was a warder from Portland Convict Prison in charge of John Lee, convict on ticket-of-leave. John Lee handed his ticket to the police officer who read it. What was it that made the policeman start as he read? What was it that made him look so curiously at the tall, thin, clean-shaven elderly man before him? It was this: Certain particulars on the ticket showed that on 4 February 1885 the bearer was sentenced to death at Exeter Assizes for murder at Babbacombe. The man was 'Babbacombe' Lee.

'Babbacombe' Lee was on his way to spend Christmas with his aged mother - John Lee, the man they could not hang, the man under whose feet the grim mechanism of the scaffold three times mysteriously failed in its appointed work.

(From Lee's autobiography)

JOHN LEE'S HOMECOMING

John Lee returned home to 3 Town Cottage, Abbotskerswell, for an emotional reunion with his elderly mother, more than twenty-three years after his arrest.

At the outset of his sentence in 1885, Lee had hoped to serve no more than fifteen years and be free by the turn of the century. It must have come as a hard blow therefore that he had still not been released when his father died in 1902.

His parents tirelessly campaigned for their son's release during his confinement, and made the long journeys to Portsmouth and Portland Prisons to see him, even though visits were permitted for only thirty minutes, once every three months. In 1894, Mr Lee wrote to Mr C Seale-Hayne, explaining that he was a poor man and the cost of the prison visits was prohibitive. He asked the MP's assistance in obtaining permission to make just one visit a year for one hour. The letter was passed to the Home Secretary, who flatly turned down the request.

Following the death of her husband, Mary Lee continued the fight alone on behalf of her son with heartfelt pleas to the Home Secretary:

> *I humbly beg mercy from you towards my dear son John Lee that has been confined in His Majesty's Prison for over 20 years as he has had such a good record and I do humbly beg for mercy under the new criminal Law for a father's feeling towards my Dear son and his poor old aged mother, a poor old broken hearted widow.*
>
> . . . . . .
>
> *Now, after existing in prison from young manhood to middle age, he was free, and with his delighted and thankful mother at Abbotskerswell. That night and the following day a little army of journalists from Torquay, Newton Abbot, Plymouth, Exeter and London invaded Abbotskerswell, to interview either Mrs Lee or her son or both, but even when Mrs Lee could be seen she refused to have anything to say.*

John Lee's homecoming

> *'Well, Mrs Lee, what can you tell me?'* queried a London pressman.
> *'Nothing,'* replied Mrs Lee.
> *'Nothing?'*
> *'Nothing.'*
> *'Sure?'*
> *'Sure.'*

Lee and his mother

So it was to all as to one - save the representative of one London newspaper, which, it is said, despatched to Abbotskerswell post-haste an emissary to buy Lee's exclusive story. *(Torquay Directory)*

Lloyd's Weekly News, a Sunday newspaper with a circulation of 1 ¼ million, secured the rights to publish Lee's story, for a fee rumoured to be £4,000. The serialisation began on 29 December 1907, eleven days after Lee's release from prison, and *The Man They Could Not Hang* became a bestseller when republished in book form as Lee's 'autobiography' in 1908.

Lee's autobiography

The first Sunday instalment brought floods of letters from well-wishers who were convinced by his pleas of innocence. Many of the writers referred to stories they had read about ' the cook's confession', a syndicated article which had surfaced in 1887, and implied that Lee's half-sister, Elizabeth Harris, had made a death-bed statement clearing him.

Lee travelled to London on 25 January 1908, writing to one of his well-wishers:

> *I am going to London, trying to find out about the confession of the cook, I do hope that I can trace it back. Dear Sir, 23 years ago no-one thought to see me again, but man proposes but God disposes. I thank you again for your kind letter and I pray to God to bless you always.*

Lee devoted a chapter of his book to his impressions of the capital and the changes and technological advances which had occurred during his incarceration. The main purpose of his visit, however, was to seek out one of the well-wishers who had told him about his half-sister's confession, showing that only one month after his release he was prepared to trace evidence

A letter from Lee showing his gratitude to well-wishers

that would clear his name, through a correspondent who knew only what he had read in the newspapers. After this and further investigation he wrote to the Home Office:

I know I have the public sympathy on my side, the greater part believe that I am an innocent man unjustly punished, in fact I am a living monument of English injustice. Being an innocent man I hope before many weeks to get the confession of my step-sister Elizabeth Harris the cook who confessed to the crime on her death bed to Major Pearson a Salvation Army Officer.

The Home Office investigated this claim but found that Pearson had died six years earlier; furthermore the Salvation Army knew nothing of these claims.

HOME OFFICE LICENSEE A60789

The Police Station Record

Prisoners freed after serving a life-sentence could be deprived of their liberty if they broke any of the conditions of their release. Lee was required to make an honest living and avoid association with the criminal classes. He was also required to report in person once a month to Newton Abbot Police Station, where details of his punctuality, character and employment were recorded. As the Station Record shows, he was allowed to report by letter after three months, and in August 1908, the Home Secretary granted him exemption from this procedure as a whole.

Lee's police report reveals that he did not gain regular employment. This was unnecessary as he had received a generous sum from a newspaper publisher for his 'story' and also sold signed photographs of himself. The Home Office was concerned about the intense press interest in Lee, but realised they were powerless to prevent Lee's story from being published, and hoped it would cause no more than a passing sensation. Another condition was imposed on Lee however, which prevented him cashing in further on his celebrity status. Prior to his release, a York impresario had announced that he was prepared to pay Lee £100 a week to tour the music halls with former executioner James Berry. The Home Office was understandably perturbed at the prospect of this 'double act' re-enacting the scene of the scaffold. Therefore, to uphold the dignity of the law, they decreed that Lee, *'shall not take part in any public performance or deliver any lecture or speech, or in any way exhibit himself at any meeting, assembly, or place of entertainment.'*

JOHN LEE STARTS A NEW LIFE

Two months after his release from prison, Lee announced his engagement, in February 1908, to Jessie Bulled, aged thirty-two. The daughter of a retired naval officer, the bride-to-be was employed as head attendant of the female wards at the Union Workhouse, Newton Abbot.

The couple were married by special license at Newton Abbot Congregational Church on Friday 22 January 1909. To avoid unwanted publicity, the ceremony was shrouded in secrecy, the only witnesses present being the pastor, registrar, church treasurer and caretaker. Local newspapers reported that a small group of friends waited outside the church and showered the newlyweds with confetti as they left for Newton Abbot railway station and boarded a train to Bristol, en route for Durham or York.

It was believed that the groom had taken a business, and he described himself on the marriage certificate as a 'proprietor of general stores'. However, no one was

Dressed for the big occasion?

talking, least of all the bride's parents who were said to be 'broken-hearted', nor John Lee's mother who refused to admit that her son had been married. Maintaining a cryptic silence, her only remark was, *'People say so, but then they said so once before.'*

THE LAST FAREWELL?

In August 1909, Lee returned to Abbotskerswell to spend his 45th birthday with his mother. During his visit, in what was his last-known interview, he told the *Mid-Devon Times:*
Fortune has been very kind to me and I have done better than I could have expected. I have been glad to meet some of my old friends in Newton Abbot but I shall not come back to this part of the country again if I can help it.

'Fortune has been very kind to me and I have done better than I could have expected.'

John Lee was about to become a father: his son John Aubrey Maurice was born in Newcastle upon Tyne on 10 January 1910. At about this time Lee was working for Wears and Watson, who owned two pubs in Newgate Street - The Bull and Mouth and The Chancellor's Head. Under the terms of his release, Lee could not make public appearances, so he was employed as a 'barman'. He was paid £8 a week, considerably more than the average wage at the time, and his drawing power was enormous. People flocked to meet and to shake hands with 'the man they could not hang'.

Despite his earlier statement, Lee made a further visit to his mother in September 1910. He was now living in London, making personal appearances at Ye Olde King's Head, a public house near London Bridge. A few months later, allegedly accompanied by a barmaid, he abandoned his wife, who was expecting their second child. In February 1911, he went to America and after sending help for some weeks he wrote stating he was out of work and could send no more money. His daughter Eveline Victoria Mary Lee was born on 10 August 1911, and on St

Ye Olde King's Head, Southwark, London

Valentine's day 1912, Jessie Lee was compelled to seek relief from the Lambeth Guardians. She told the Board that her husband had previously held a situation in the borough and received a good salary for 'exhibiting' himself. What became of John Lee after this date is a mystery that has been the subject of much conjecture.

PART 2

CHAPTER 6 THE RISE AND FALL OF THE GLEN

The Glen with the Garden Room (right) and colonnade

The details of the tragedy which was enacted at the isolated little villa on the beach at Babbacombe early on the morning of Saturday, the 15th of November last, are so fresh in the minds of the public generally that there is no necessity for repeating them beyond giving a brief outline. Miss Keyse, the lady who met with her death at the hands of John Lee, was nearly seventy years of age. She was the daughter of Mrs. Whitehead by a former marriage [Emma's father had died in 1821], and resided nearly all her lifetime at the house now known as the Glen. It is only within the last twelve months or two years that the house has been known by this name, having always been previously known as "Babbacombe." The change made in the name of the place was the cause of some correspondence between Miss Keyse and Mr. Tollemache, who had already given that title to his house situated higher up the valley. But all through the trial Miss Keyse's house was referred to as "The Glen," and probably in future it will always be known as such.

This *Torquay Directory* article appeared at the time of the murder and reveals that Mr Tollemache, owner of the other Glen, now the site of the Glen Hotel, was somewhat aggrieved when Miss Keyse began calling her home The Glen. At the time of her death The Glen was still generally known as 'Babbacombe', though it had originally been called 'Beach House' when built by W Davey in 1812. Adjoining The Glen was The Music Room, also known as the Garden Room, reached through a colonnade, both of which can be seen in the photograph.

The tragic circumstances surrounding the death of Miss Keyse led to the gradual demise of The Glen estate and the eventual disappearance of all her property. The interest in the 'Babbacombe Murder' however, in no way diminished and a journalist later observed, *'What an opportunity somebody missed in omitting to preserve the cottage as a show-place for visitors.'*

The Glen occupied a prime site on Babbacombe Beach and commanded a panoramic view of the surrounding coastline. On a clear day it was possible to see Portland Bill, where John Lee served the greater part of his prison sentence.

The estate stretched from Babbacombe Downs at the top of the cliff, encompassing all the land to one side of the winding path which descended down a steep decline to the charming marine villa. On the opposite side of the path alongside The Glen was the Cary Arms Inn, named after the family who were Lords of the Manor. Ornamental gardens and manicured lawns in the grounds of The Glen contrasted with the rough terrain that had to be negotiated to reach the top of the hill, and it was impossible for vehicles to reach the beach. The coffin of Emma Keyse was carried up the track by local fishermen to meet the cortege waiting on the Downs road.

During Emma Keyse's lifetime, The Glen had enjoyed an enviable reputation for hospitality. Her mother, Elizabeth Whitehead, hosted lavish social gatherings, and Princess Victoria took tea in the gracious surroundings of the Garden Room. The *Torquay Times* described how this extension also contained ten bedrooms and a music room to entertain visitors:

The revenue cutters used frequently to put into Babbacombe, and the officers The Garden Room
were the guests of Mrs Whitehead. In order that there might be every accommodation for pleasure parties, a separate building was constructed as a dancing room, with a covered way from the living premises.

Princess Victoria and her mother, the Duchess of Kent, paid a visit to The Glen in 1833. This was the first of many royal visits to Babbacombe made by the future queen and members of the Royal Family.

The Lithograph of Babbacombe Bay showing the Royal Yacht (centre)

It is often claimed that Emma Keyse was a lady-in-waiting or a matron of honour to Queen Victoria, but a descendant of the Keyse family found no reference to any such association in the Buckingham Palace records. Her mother, Elizabeth, had royal connections and acted as governess to the infant Princess Victoria when the Royal Family visited Sidmouth in 1819. It is also thought that another relative of Emma Keyse was a tutor to the Prince of Wales, the future King Edward VII.

When she became queen, Victoria visited Babbacombe Bay on two more occasions, but did not come ashore. Staying aboard the Royal Yacht, she sketched the scenery and wrote in her journal that it was a beautiful spot, with wooded hills *'reminding one of a ballet or play where nymphs appear'*.

William Gasking, landlord of the Cary Arms at the time of the Babbacombe Murder, presented a lithograph to the Royal Consort, Prince Albert when he visited Babbacombe in 1852. The scene shows the Royal Yacht flanked by the *Black Eagle* and the *Fairy* drawn when Queen Victoria and Prince Albert sailed to the Bay in 1846.

Gasking died in 1896 and a year later the new landlord of the Cary Arms, Alexander Lorimer, produced a souvenir to commemorate Queen Victoria's Diamond Jubilee, recording the Royal visits to Babbacombe. The reference to the visit made by the Prince of Wales however, is incorrect and actually occurred on 5 September 1878; not on 5 August 1879.

John Lee narrowly missed meeting Royalty. In his autobiography, he claimed that he first obtained work with Miss Keyse a few days after his 15th birthday in August 1879 and stayed for 18 months before joining the Navy. This ghost-written account, told nearly 30 years after the event, is inaccurate, as Lee enlisted on the 1 October 1879, only six weeks after his birthday. It is more likely that he was employed at the age of 14, shortly following the Prince of Wales's visit to The Glen in September 1878.

Lee also described how, in May 1880, while he was in the Navy, the Prince of Wales presented half a sovereign to each of the servants at The Glen, including his half-sister, Elizabeth Harris. In actual fact, his sister Millie was cook at this time, and was not replaced by Elizabeth until 1882.

A. LORIMER, CARY ARMS HOTEL,
Proprietor. BABBACOMBE.

In kind Remembrance of the Jubilee Year of . .
Her most Gracious Majesty the Queen.

The Landlord of the "Cary Arms Inn," will supply to his
Customers this Summer, a Copy of this Record of the Dates of
the Visits to Babbicombe by Members of the Royal Family.　.

1ST AUGUST, 1833—The Duchess of Kent, with her daughter the Princess Victoria,
landed at Torquay, and after a brief stay at the Royal Hotel, paid a visit to Mrs. Whitehead
at Babbicombe.

AUGUST, 1846—The Royal Squadron, with Her most Gracious Majesty the Queen and
Prince Albert and others on board, anchored in the Bay.

ON MONDAY, JULY 19TH, 1852—At three o'clock p.m., the Royal Squadron was
observed by the preventive men on the heights at Babbicombe steering for Torquay;
bearing 20 to 25 miles S.E. The active Coastguards at Babbicombe were immediately
numbered in their uniforms, and were soon afloat in a fine boat to do honor to the Royal
Standard of England. As soon as the boat was seen by the Squadron, the Royal Yacht
altered its course, and soon came within hail. His Royal Highness Prince Albert and his
Private Secretary, stepped into the boat and were immediately pulled on shore. The
excitement among the inhabitants of the beautiful hamlet of Babbicombe was immense, and
they crowded the shore and every part of the hills to give expression to their feelings of
loyalty. Mrs. Whitehead received the Royal party as they landed, and Mr. Gasking, the
proprietor of the beautiful hotel, the "Cary Arms" which is so picturesquely situated at the
foot of the cliff, caused mahogany planks to be laid down to facilitate the passage of the
Royal party over the beach.

His Royal Highness walked to the top of the hill, where he engaged a carriage belonging
to Henry Manning, coach proprietor of St. Mary Church, requesting to be driven to the
principal parts of Torquay. His Royal Highness went through the New Terrace Drive from
Torquay by Meadfoot to Babbicombe .Hill, where an immense number of persons had
assembled to show respect to the Consort of our beloved Queen. Miss Keyse had the honor
of conducting the Prince through the celebrated grounds of Mrs. Whitehead, with which his
Royal Highness expressed himself highly gratified.

During the time Prince Albert was thus employed, the Prince of Wales and his brother
landed with Captain Crispin, and were engaged in examining and enjoying the beauties of
Mrs. Whitehead's house and grounds.

At the request of Her Majesty, Lieutenant Sharp, of the Coastguard Service, went on
board the Royal Yacht, and was graciously requested to steer the Barge along the coast, the
scenery of which was much admired, and sketches were taken of some of the point most
interesting. The urbanity of the Royal party was the delight of all who had the pleasure of
enjoying an intercourse so unexpected and so novel.

On the Royal party leaving Babbicombe, Mr. Gasking, of the "Cary Arms" had the
honor of presenting the Princes with a lithograph view of Babbicombe, taken in 1846, when
Her Majesty graciously anchored in the Bay, and the Royal Squadron is seen at anchor.

AUGUST 5TH, 1879—Another visit of His Royal Highness the Prince of Wales, who
took tea at the "Cary Arms," accompanied by Lord Charles Beresford and party.

MAY 18TH, 1880—Another visit by their Royal Highnesses, the Prince and Princess of
Wales, and two sons, Prince Albert Victor of Wales and Prince George Frederick of Wales,
and the Duchess of Sutherland.

1897 souvenir to commemorate Queen Victoria's Diamond Jubilee

The view of Babbacombe which Queen Victoria enjoyed sketching. The Glen is on the beach with the Garden Room and Boathouse on the right and the Cary Arms Inn on the left. High above The Glen is The Vine, also owned by Emma Keyse's family

The Glen in its prime

Emma Keyse was proud of her royal connections and Lee revealed that The Glen's largest bedroom, the Honeysuckle room, was known in the household as *'the Queen's room, because the Royal yacht once put in at Babbacombe, and the room was prepared for Queen Victoria in case she wanted it'*.

In April 1885 the entire contents of The Glen were put on sale. This presented an ideal opportunity for the public to inspect the scene of the crime, and souvenir-hunters jostled with dealers. The Auctioneers charged 1s-0d for admission by catalogue in an attempt to discourage the merely curious, but this proved to be no deterrent. Several hundred people turned up and long queues developed. The auction lasted two days and was eventually concluded outside The Glen on Babbacombe Beach.

Furniture, paintings, books, china and silver all went under the hammer at knock-down prices. John Lee's fold-up bed was sold along with other items from the pantry, some for exhibition purposes, although there was disappointment that no representative from Madame Tussaud's attended, despite the fact that John Lee's image was to be displayed at the famous waxworks.

The elderly retainers, Eliza and Jane Neck, were in attendance at the sale, and continued to live at The Glen stripped of all its furnishings until Eliza died at the age of 74, in December 1886. Jane, two years younger, survived until April 1891, spending her last years at Princes St, Babbacombe, with the family of fisherman Thomas Stiggins, a nephew of William Gasking, who had previously rented a cottage from Miss Keyse on Babbacombe Beach.

Fire-damage to The Glen had been estimated at £100, but it was never restored, and a lucrative tourist attraction was overlooked and eventually demolished. Local businessmen however were quick to spot other potential sources of revenue. Souvenirs of the tragedy were on offer a few days after the murder and newspapers published special supplements. Competition was fierce amongst local photographers. Mr Kitto advertised 'The Only View Of The House, including the broken dining room windows'. Pierce's Photographic Studio boasted 'The Latest Photograph of John Lee - acknowledged the best likeness out' which brought the following warning from Mr Collis, the owner of the original negative, 'the public are cautioned against purchasing Vile and Spurious Copies of the prisoner John Lee'.

The award for enterprise however belongs to the Babbacombe barmaid who found an old piece of rope on the beach outside The Glen, and sold strands of it to guillible visitors, claiming it was from the noose that failed to hang John Lee. The executors of Emma Keyse estate made an unsuccessful attempt to auction The Glen on August 29, 1889. The property had once been on the market valued at £16,000, but it now failed to attract a bid in advance of £2,000.

An advertisement placed by the auctioneers, Williams & Cox gives a graphic description of the splendour of the 13-acre estate. The principal residence described is The Vine, built in 1820, which had been used by Miss Keyse to accommodate visitors. Her former home is referred to by its original name, Beach House. It is evident that it was not expected that anyone would wish to reside in the building where the murder took place as permission had been granted to, 'erect a house - in substitution for the Cottage immediately above the beach'.

TO YACHTSMEN AND OTHERS.

BABBACOMBE,

TORQUAY, DEVON.

For SALE by PUBLIC AUCTION, a singularly beautiful

MARINE RESIDENCE

called "Beach House," and "The Vine," but commonly known as

THE GLEN

occupying one of the loveliest situations on the Coast of Devon, and unequalled in its attractions as a Yachting Station.

It is within two miles of Torquay; about two miles and a half from the Railway Station, and within five minutes' walk of the Church, Post Office, Shops, and the Golf Ground.

This Property has been several times visited and greatly admired by the Queen and other members of the Royal Family.

The GROUNDS comprise the whole of one side of a most picturesque Glen, and extend to the sea shore. They are of singular beauty, and are well planted and tastefully laid out in Shrubberies, woodland and wilderness walks, with winding paths leading to secluded nooks, commanding magnificent views of Coast Scenery extending to Portland Bill, as well as of the far-famed Babbacombe Bay. There are also lawns suitable for Croquet or Tennis, Kitchen or other Gardens.

The principal RESIDENCE stands on a level Plateau at a good elevation in a sheltered and charming situation. It contains lofty Hall, Drawing and Dining Rooms, each 27 feet in length; Breakfast Room, Nine Bed Rooms, and Man Servant's Room, good Kitchen and Offices; 3-Stalled Stable, Loft, and Coach House. Hard and Soft Waters are laid on. There is also a Cottage situated on small level Lawn immediately above the Beach, approached by Colonnade, and containing Entrance Hall, Dining Room, pretty Ante-Room, Conservatory, leading to a Drawing Room; handsome Music or Billiard Room, 34ft. x 19ft. 6in. (detached), but connected with a main Building by a covered passage; Ten Bed Rooms and Dressing Rooms, Kitchen Offices, and extensive Cellarage.

On the Beach is a large BOAT HOUSE with Three Rooms over. The Property affords exceptional advantages for Yachting, there being good anchorage with deep water close in shore; landing is easy at all times of the tide, and the new Pier or Breakwater which is now being erected at Babbacombe will provide ample shelter for a Boat of moderate size. There is good Sea Fishing, and the Bathing is excellent.

The Grounds include several valuable BUILDING SITES, and there is the right to erect a House, without increase of Ground Rent in substitution for the Cottage immediately above the Beach, and a Lodge for the House. The Ground Landlord is willing to allow further Building if desired, on terms to be agreed on between him and the Owner of the Premises for Sale.

The Property is held from R. S. CARY, Esq., on Three Leases from Sept. 29th, 1888, renewable for ever on payment of Fines and Heriots, as follow: The First Lease which comprises the position abutting on the sea shore, is on Three Lives, aged respectively 79, 40, and 24 years; Fine £93, Heriot £5. The Second, which includes the upper house and Grounds, is held on three lives, aged respectively 51, 40, and 24 years; Fine £50, Heriot £3 3s. The Third Lease, which comprises the portion of Land above the House and adjoining Babbacombe Down, is also hold on Three Lives, aged respectively 24, 8, and 4 years; Fine £60, Heriot £5.

These pictures were taken before and after The Glen was demolished in 1894

A buyer was eventually found and Frederick Way took over The Glen Estate in October 1890. He and his family moved into The Vine which was renamed Glen Sannox. The Glen was demolished in 1894.

The beach café (above) and the café and Boathouse after the fire (below)

In the 1920s, The Glen Estate, now renamed Babbacombe Court was purchased for £7,300 by Torquay Borough Council and the Garden Room converted into a beach café. A week after opening for Easter in April 1928, the café and the adjoining Boathouse were completely destroyed by fire.

The new beach café

A new beach café was opened in 1930 and the town council considered various plans for the remainder of the Estate. It was proposed that Babbacombe Court be sold and the proceeds used to lay out gardens as a pleasureground for the public. Alternatively, it was thought the house should become a museum. Following decades of indecision, the house became a derelict ruin and was demolished in 1960. The only reminder of The Glen was a wine cellar pictured on a period postcard.

JOHN LEE'S CELLAR

Underground wine cellar forming part of BABBACOMBE BEACH CAFE, only remaining part of original house which was the scene in 1884 of the Babbacombe Beach murder.

John Lee, a pantry boy, was sentenced to death for the murder of Miss Keyse, his employer.

After three attempts to hang him had failed he was given a life sentence ; the case subsequently becoming known as " The John Lee murder ; the man they could not hang."

This cellar survived until 1974 when the café was demolished

PART 3

CHAPTER 7 JOHN LEE: EXPLODING THE MYTHS

Innumerable newspaper and journal articles have been written about John Lee, perpetuating the myths that surround the Babbacombe Murder. Yet, despite such speculation, four mysteries remain unanswered concerning the life of John Lee. The final part of this book examines each of these:

● The differing versions of Lee's whereabouts in his later life and the unsubstantiated accounts of his death occurring in four separate countries.

● The numerous theories - including bribery, collusion, weather conditions and even witchcraft - that have been offered to explain why the execution of John Lee failed.

● Allegations that Lee's mother was once accused of child murder, and was acquitted only after turning Queen's evidence against her co-defendant in another infamous Torquay murder mystery - the Charlotte Winsor case.

● The suspicion that someone else was implacated in the crime. This suspicion has existed since newspapers of the day, including this account in the *Western Morning News*, recorded: *A report is current, and is not altogether without foundation, that when John Lee is brought up for further examination before the magistrates - he will not be the only occupant of the prisoner's dock.* Did Lee cover up for the real killer? Could it have been the smuggler, the builder, the silver dealer, the fisherman, or the lover of Elizabeth Harris? The possible identity of the latter produces a twist to the plot that would grace a novel by the late Torquay-born mystery writer Agatha Christie.

JOHN LEE 1864 - ?

The trail left by John Lee following his departure from London in 1911 has proved extremely elusive and the site of his final resting place is complete conjecture. Conflicting tales of his whereabouts started to emerge following the death of his devoted mother who, according to the *Torquay Times*, *'held firmly to the belief of his innocence to the last day of her life'*.

Mary Lee died on 18 March 1918, aged 86. Her funeral was not attended by any of her children. Elizabeth Harris never contacted her family after her half-brother's trial, and Amelia Lee did not survive either of her parents. The first person named in Mary Lee's will, made in January 1915, was her deserted

Mary Lee

daughter-in-law Jessie Lee, to whom she left half her clothes, a silver teapot, six cups and saucers, and the family bible. Small bequests were made to her landlord and two of her nieces before mentioning her errant son:

I give all the rest of my property subject to the payment of my just debts, funeral and testamentary expenses to my son John Henry George Lee but if he shall be abroad at the time of my death then I direct that the same shall be sold and the proceeds forwarded to him.

Soon after his mother's death, newspapers announced that Lee had died in Melbourne, Australia, where a film of his life was enjoying great success. Similar stories surfaced in Canada in 1921 with claims that he had died after a career as a gold prospector. He was also said to have been posted to London with the Canadian army in 1917, which at the age of 53 would have made Lee the oldest serving conscript.

In 1922 the *Torquay Times* attached no relevance to these earlier disclosures and stated that Lee had last been heard of in Buffalo, USA. The 1920 Census for New York State certainly reveals that an Englishman called John Lee was living in Buffalo, although he was the head of a large family and thirteen years older than his infamous namesake.

JOHN LEE - THE MOVIE

Late in 1912, a film *The Man They Could Not Hang* was produced in Australia, probably inspired by John Lee's autobiography and a stage play that had appeared earlier that year. The film was considered technically crude, even by the standards of early silent movies, having cost less than £300 to make, and was described (in 1921) by one Australian critic as 'about the worst ever'. It was directed by a young actor, Philip Scott, whose main memory of the low budget production was the cramped conditions of the 'studio': 'It was really only a room, fitted out like a photographer's.'

The producer, Phillip Lytton, shelved the picture and eventually presented it to a former employee, Arthur W Sterry. Sterry and his partner, Frederick Haldane, enjoyed great success with the feature when it went on general release in 1917, making an estimated £50,000 out of the venture. They then produced a second version in 1921 which, like its predecessor, received scathing reviews but proved to be a huge box-office attraction.

Frederick Haldane toured Britain with the film during 1923-25 and many people believe that John Lee made personal appearances at cinemas where it was shown. This

EMPIRE

NEWTON ABBOT.

Whit-Week, May 21st. For Six Days.
TWICE DAILY AT 3 AND 7-45.

THE LIFE STORY OF JOHN LEE.

The Man they-
could not hang

The Picture will be Graphically described by
FREDERICK HALDANE or W. J. MACKAY.

VOCAL ITEMS by
LOUIE FARNDON or ELOISE MILLER

Specially arranged Orchestral Music and Effects.

Special Prices: 1/10, 1/3, 1/- (Tax included)

certainly was not the case at theatres in London, Manchester, Cardiff or Bradford. Many of Lee's relatives saw the film when it appeared at Newton Abbot in May 1923, but there was no celebrity in attendance. Haldane spent a day in the company of a local journalist viewing sights in the area connected with Lee, including Babbacombe Beach, but evidently had never met Lee as he made no reference to any personal association with the subject of his film. The reporter who interviewed Haldane opined that Lee had died having gone 'to America and drifted to Australia'.

The Sydney actor Haldane, or one of his team, gave a passionate lecture from the stage during the screening, and often simulated the voices of the characters, a technique described as the first 'Speaking Moving Picture'. Therefore, cinema-goers who later recalled shaking hands with John Lee, dressed as a convict, or hearing him describe the execution, had in all probability seen one of the performers. It has also been suggested that Lee acted as 'adviser' during production of the 1912 film. This again is highly unlikely.

There have been numerous claims that John Lee returned to England, and a Home Office memo written in 1916 mentioned that Lee had recently been spotted in Brighton, while a wartime police-sergeant revealed that Lee often used to call into a London sub-station for a chat, bemoaning his (Lee's) fate at the hands of the establishment. At the end of hostilities in 1918, an army officer believed that Lee was running a second-hand furniture shop in Plymouth. Two years later, Lee was said to be doing odd-jobs in Derby, where a colliery manager remembered paying him one shilling for cutting his hedge. Lancashire cinema-goers were convinced  that, in the 1920s, Lee appeared with the film of his life in the towns of Blackburn, Failsworth, Middleton and Salford.

Searches at the General Register Office have established that there is no record of Lee's death during the 1930s which positively identifies him, although there are several claims that he died during this period at Abbotskerswell, Durham, London, and even by his own hand at Plymouth. Lee did consider adopting his mother's maiden name to avoid the glare of publicity, and it is possible he chose this option, even though he had found that the name 'Babbacombe' Lee could at least guarantee an income.

One thing is certain: even John Lee could not escape the inevitable, though according to one story he cheated death yet again during the London Blitz. Rescued from the rubble of his bombed-out shop in Paddington, the old man smiled as an anxious policeman helped him to his feet and declared, 'That was a narrow escape, you're lucky to be alive!'

MURDER: AN HEREDITARY TRAIT ?

The news that John Lee had died in Milwaukee in 1933 was widely believed, though as with earlier reports, never substantiated. However, the death of Isidore Carter in February 1936 appeared to sever the final link with the Babbacombe Murder, but immediately raised questions about John Lee's parentage.

Isidore Carter

Carter was Emma Keyse's solicitor, and acted for the prosecution at Lee's trial. In his obituary published in the Torquay *Herald Express*, his law partner Mr C Field-Fisher 'reluctantly' revealed that Carter had always upheld privately that John Lee was the son of Mary Jane Harris, a woman whom Carter had persuaded to turn Queen's evidence against co-defendant Charlotte Winsor, who was subsequently convicted of child murder.

Field-Fisher's startling revelation infers that both mother and son stood trial for murder, but a cursory examination of the facts reveals otherwise. Mary Lee (neé Harris) was married to John Lee senior and lived at Abbotskerswell, while *Mary Jane* Harris lodged in Torquay, and her child was fathered by a farmer called Nickells. Mary Lee gave birth to John in August 1864, two months before Mary Jane Harris's son Thomas was born. Thomas Harris was murdered by Charlotte Winsor in December 1864, when John Lee was four months old.

It is evident that Mary Lee and Mary Jane Harris were not one and the same person, and it is interesting to note that Field-Fisher did not repeat these claims in 1948, when he lectured on the subject of Carter's involvement in the murder trial. The myth was perpetuated, however, and although John Lee was born several months before Mary Jane Harris was arrested, one writer was moved to speculate that if the story in Carter's obituary was correct and Lee was indeed Mary Jane Harris's son, 'She must have become pregnant while she was in prison, and at a time when Carter himself was seeing her frequently'.

CHAPTER 8 THE EXECUTION OF JOHN LEE - THEREBY HANGS A TALE!

The name of John Lee would not have passed into folklore without the extraordinary events that occurred at Exeter Prison on Monday 23 February 1885. Three times he was placed on the scaffold, the noose placed around his neck and the bolt drawn by a lever to activate the drop, but each time the trap-doors mysteriously failed to open, though they worked perfectly when he stepped off the trap. The execution was abandoned and the prisoner led away. A legend was born, spawning numerous theories as to why Lee's life had been spared.

PROVIDENCE

It is evident from letters written to his family from the condemned cell that Lee's religious beliefs greatly sustained him throughout the trial and the days leading up to the death sentence. Later, he firmly believed that he had been saved by divine intervention, and this was borne out by his remarkable dream on the eve of the execution. The dream turned out to be an exact account of what happened and was later recounted in full by the Prison Chaplain in a letter to Lord Clinton, who was the Chairman of the Exeter Quarter Sessions.

> *'After the attempted execution of Lee on February 23rd 1885 I went to his cell and spoke to him about the extraordinary event that had happened to him. He replied that on the night before his execution he had a dream which had shown him what would happen. At my request he related it to me. He said that in his dream he saw himself being led from his cell down through the reception basement to the scaffold which was just outside the basement door. He saw himself placed upon the scaffold and efforts being made to force the drop, which, however, would not work. He then saw himself led away from the place of execution, since it was decided that a new scaffold would have to be built before the sentence of the law could be carried out. He told me that when he woke at six o'clock on the morning fixed for his execution he had mentioned the dream to the two officers who were in the cell with him.'*

The two warders, James Milford and Samuel Bennett, had reported the dream to the Prison Governor. The Reverend Pitkin enclosed a copy of their statement with his letter:

> *'At six a.m., when John Lee rose from his bed, he said, "Mr Bennett, I have dreamed a very singular and strange dream. I thought the time was come, and I was led down through the reception out into the hanging place, but when they placed me on the drop they could not hang me, for there was something wrong with the machinery of the drop. They then took me off from the drop and took me (instead of the way I had come) around the A Wing, and back through the A Ward to my cell."'*

These events, together with the story that a white dove had appeared above the scaffold, added credence to Lee's reply to the trial Judge who commented on how calmly the prisoner had reacted as the death sentence was passed:

> *'The reason my Lord, why I am so calm and collected is because I trust in my Lord, and he knows that I am innocent.'*

John Lee was not the only member of his family to have a prophetic dream on the eve of the execution. His parents went to bed late hoping to sleep through the fateful hour of eight o'clock. They were kept awake by a strange knocking sound on the bedroom wall. A table by the bedside shook, causing a candlestick to fall off. The candle broke in two, but remained alight. When at last the couple fell into a fitful sleep, Mary Lee had a strange dream. She saw her son on the scaffold, the bolt was drawn, but the rope broke, and the body fell to the bottom of a pit.

WITCHCRAFT

The Devil emerged as an alternative to Providence as people sought an explanation for Lee's escape from the jaws of death.

John Lee's mother was said to have visited a church graveyard on the eve of the execution and recited the Lord's Prayer backwards to summon the Evil One to save her son, while Granny Lee of Ogwell told locals, 'They shall not hang him' as she walked to Exeter on the morning of the execution and kept a vigil from a spot overlooking the prison. A further story revealed that a white witch was paid handsomely by friends of Lee to save him from hanging.

In his autobiography, Lee poured scorn on such tales, but the witchcraft theory gained support from a surprising source. The Archdeacon of Westminster reported to the Home Secretary that he knew the Lees well and they were a well-known witch family on Dartmoor.

Act of God or sorcery, the editor of *The Times* was fiercely critical of the Home Secretary's decision to reprieve Lee and anticipated that his action would, 'encourage foolish and superstitious people to believe, in spite of evidence as clear as noonday, that Lee was wrongfully convicted.'

INCOMPETENCE

Hanging in the nineteenth century had not acquired the proficiency later attained by the Billingtons and the Pierrepoints. Despite stories to the contrary, a dummy was not used to test the gallows with weight. This practice only became customary following the failure of Lee's execution. A warder was lowered through the trap door during the abortive attempts to find the fault, but as a reporter noted at the time, he did not stand on the trap in the same way as the prisoner. John Lee was by no means the first condemned prisoner to walk away from the scaffold, nor was he the first to survive three attempts. The original 'man they could not hang' was Londoner Joseph Samuel who gained a reprieve in Australia in 1801, when two ropes broke and a third slowly unravelled, rendering him unconscious.

The hangman, James Berry suffered embarrassment at several other executions. The length of rope required to break the neck and bring about instantaneous death was based on tables he used, which took into consideration the age, weight and build of the prisoner. Miscalculations of the 'long drop' by Berry often resulted in death by slow strangulation, while other unfortunates had their heads partly severed by the rope.

A few months after the bungled execution at Exeter, Berry officiated at a particularly grisly scene at Norwich Prison. In November 1885, Robert Goodale had his head completely sliced off by the rope. This incident led to an official enquiry into the methods of hanging in England.

Berry's exploits came to the notice of Queen Victoria who reminded the Home Secretary, 'since this new executioner has taken it in hand, there have been several accidents'. The day after Lee's execution, Earl Cowper, father of Lord Mount-Temple, a close neighbour of Emma Keyse, rose in the House of Lords and proposed that a full-time public executioner should be appointed to replace freelance hangmen like Berry, suggesting, 'it would be easier to get a good man for a permanent place of, say, £200 or £300 a year'.

Commenting unfavourably on Lee's reprieve, the editor of *The Times* also targeted Berry for criticism, by asking, 'is it right that an executioner's blunder should return to such a being the life that he has lawfully forfeited?'

A SLICE OF MISFORTUNE

The appalling scene with John Lee produced apprehension in prisons all over the country, especially when James Berry was officiating.

In November 1885, the executioner arrived at Norwich Castle to carry out the hanging of wife murderer, Robert Goodale, and found the prison staff in a state of sheer panic. It transpired that one of the warders had experienced a recurring dream, in which he had seen Goodale beheaded instead of hanged! The warder told Berry he had had the dream three times and urged him to tell the authorities that it was inadvisable to proceed.

Berry was anxious after his earlier experience with Lee, but did not believe in dreams and omens. Furthermore he had no wish to call off the execution and lose his fee. What followed was one of the most horrific botch-ups in the annals of British hangings, graphically described by Berry in his memoirs.

'When I pulled the lever the drop fell properly and the prisoner dropped out of sight. We were horrified, however, to see that the rope jerked upwards and for an instant I thought the noose had slipped from the culprit's head or that the rope had broken. But it was worse than that for the jerk had severed the head entirely from the body and both had fallen into the bottom of the pit.'

CONSPIRACY

The defence counsel at Lee's trial suggested that Elizabeth Harris's lover could have been responsible for the crime and the belief has persisted that Lee covered up for that person.

One theory suggests that the father of the cook's child was a member of the nobility, and collusion of people in high places and among the Freemasons influenced officials to 'fix' the execution. Alternatively, it is believed that Harris was involved with a highly respected local businessman who bribed the executioner. James Berry found his calling abhorrent and was simply attracted by the £10 commission fee, therefore he may well have been receptive to an offer which would pay him considerably more for failing to carry out the death sentence.

The validity of these conspiracy theories appears to hinge on Lee's conviction that he would not die on the gallows. However, many other people were convinced that he would not hang. As a Torquay newspaper reported a few days after the execution:

'Fortunes have been won and lost in making spiders run across heated plates. Accordingly when Lee was arrested, bets were laid that he would not be hanged. The remarkable escape by Lee from death by accident or otherwise has been quite a wind-fall to those who laid against his being executed.'

JAMES BERRY - EXECUTIONER

Boot-salesman and former policeman who lived in Bradford, James Berry was one of a number of freelance hangmen receiving their commissions from local county sheriffs who were responsible for carrying out the sentence of the courts. Despite being opposed to capital punishment, Berry fought his conscience to execute 134 men and women between 1884 and 1892, freely admitting he did it solely for the money.

A few months after the fiasco at Exeter Prison, Berry wrote to a friend offering his hangman's rope for 25 shillings, while on another occasion, he tried to obtain the dress of an executed woman in order to sell it to Madame Tussaud's. In 1901 the escapologist 'Houdini' appeared in Bradford and Berry offered to manacle the 'Handcuff King' and share thousands of pounds in wagers if the great showman would pretend he could not escape. Houdini turned down the proposition, commenting contemptuously in his diary, *'I guess he doesn't know how I was brought up.'* James Berry

This evidence of mercenary instincts has led many to believe that Berry was 'persuaded' to bungle the execution of John Lee.

THE SCAFFOLD

Close scrutiny has been brought to bear on the apparatus used for the execution and several explanations have emerged to show why the trap-door failed. The scaffold was simply too frail for the purpose, was the conclusion reached by James Berry when he first inspected the equipment. The drop had only been used once, five years previously, for the execution of child murderer Annie Took. Berry made recommendations to the Governor for future improvements, but was confident that the apparatus would work satisfactorily on this occasion. The executioner's explanation for the failure of the drop focused on the trap-doors which were only one inch thick and needed to be three or four times as heavy. Therefore, when the prisoner stood on the trap, his weight jammed the bolts and made it impossible to draw the lever fully.

The Annual Register for 1885 attributed the failure of the drop to the fact that 'the rains of the preceding night had caused the planks to swell, and hence the trouble'. Berry himself refuted this suggestion because the doors opened satisfactorily when the prisoner was not standing on them, and attempts to saw and plane the sides of the doors to prevent them sticking did not improve the operation. In spite of Berry's protestations, the belief persisted that the British weather had been instrumental in gaining a reprieve for a condemned murderer. A Babbacombe resident poured scorn on the theory in a letter to *The Times:*

> *It appears that John Lee who broke the skull and cut the throat of his benefactress, and than set fire to her body, is not to be hanged as, owing to the rain on Sunday night, the drop did not work easily the next morning. It should be announced that in future, executions will take place weather permitting.*

The sabotage theory emerged a few years after the abortive execution. A former prisoner told the Referee that he was a member of the working party which prepared the trap-doors in the carpenter's shop.

> *The idea was conceived of inserting a flange in the sides of the flap so that any pressure exerted from above forced the flange into a slit in the adjacent woodwork. When no weight was on them the doors fell away quite easily.*

A simpler explanation came from Frank Ross, who during the First World War was working as a cleaner at Chelmsford Prison. He met a warder who claimed he had escorted Lee to the scaffold. The warder told Ross that the gallows were constructed by convict-labour, including a lifer who was a master joiner. The platform was deliberately built in such a way that, when someone (in Lee's case, the Prison Chaplain) stood on a warped board facing the prisoner, his weight flattened the board and jammed the trap.

A group of Midlands engineering apprentices proved this theory possible in the 1930s when they constructed a quarter scale model of the scaffold. A warped board inserted where the prison chaplin would have stood acted as a lock on the trap-doors when weight was applied.

A variation of this sabotage theory appeared in March 1945. A correspondent of the *Western Morning News* claimed that he read the death-bed confession of a fellow prisoner in 1920 who was the aforementioned master joiner at Lee's execution. In this version the craftsman apparently told John Lee to stand on the middle board which was warped, so that his weight would jam the trap. This revelation from Mr J R Pile of Bideford, had an intriguing postscript: '. . . according to what I read, the two men agreed that John Lee should say on the morning of the execution that he had a dream that night that he should not be hanged.' Artisan Warder Chas Edwards reported to the Governor that the failure arose 'from the iron bearing bars of the trap-doors being too light and lengthening when the weight of the body caused it to lock'. A more detailed explanation was prepared the day following the execution when Home Office officials led by Major Hardy visited Exeter Prison to inspect the scaffold. They found that when they placed a weight equivalent to that of Lee on the platform, the trap-doors would not fall. The scaffold had apparently been moved from another part of the prison in 1882 and, as was explained in their report, was out of alignment when reassembled and this was the reason it would not work properly. An extract from the report reads:

A careful examination of the scaffold was made by Messrs Libby & Cuthbert clerks of works, who visited the prison on Tuesday morning. They found the apparatus under cover in the van-house and apparently quite dry. They examined the details of the apparatus from beneath the platform. On looking at the draw bolt from the top where a board of the platform had been removed, signs of friction were apparent on the inner surface of one of the cranks in it. Believing that the bearing of the end of the hinge at this point was the cause of the failure in the machinery, they tried to move the lever with a weight equivalent to 168lbs on the platform, and the platform would not fall. They discovered that the end of one of the long hinges was resting an1/8th of an inch on the draw bolts at the crank. Then they tried to work the lever without any weight on the platform and found that when the lever was drawn quickly the platform fell. If drawn slowly, on one trial it remained fast, and on another trial it fell, but seemed to bind or grate at the end of the long hinge already referred to.

They were then perfectly satisfied that the cause of the failure to act was due to the fact that one of the long hinges rested on the draw bolt 1/8th of an inch too much. It is probable that in the refixing of the scaffold the two sides were placed 1/8th of an inch nearer than they had been before or that the long hinges had been very slightly bent in some way at the time.

The evidence is conclusive, and although providence, witchcraft, collusion, bribery and rainfall may well have played their part, the fact remains the gallows would not have worked in any case due to a simple mechanical fault.

Even this problem could have been overcome if the solution of the Sheriff of Devon had been adopted. Mr Octavius Bradshaw bore the responsibility for the failure to hang Lee, but had not attended the execution, leaving it in the hands of his deputy. Deeply embarrassed by the events, he wrote to the Home Secretary:

The sentence should have been carried out in a decent way by those who accepted the responsibility, but who appear to have entirely lost their heads. Had a few plans been used after the drop had first failed to act, or some other simple means been adopted over the drop, we should have been saved the disgrace of all the revolting bungling that took place, and the country would have been rid of a most callous and barbarous murderer.

CHAPTER 9 THE MURDER SUSPECTS

John Lee always protested he did not commit the murder of Emma Keyse: upon his arrest, during his trial, whilst imprisoned, he always denied his guilt. Even after his release from gaol he attempted to find evidence to clear his name.

If he was innocent, who was the Babbacombe Murderer? The interest in the case has produced many possible solutions, including the outlandish theory that Emma Keyse was killed because she knew too much about the affair between actress Lily Langtry and the Prince of Wales, who had visited The Glen with his wife the Princess.

This story is only one of many which have emerged to explain that fateful night at The Glen.

THE SMUGGLER

Babbacombe was a popular haunt for smugglers and John Lee was short of money, knew all the local mariners, and was ideally placed at The Glen to act as lookout and signal the all-clear to waiting ships. It is unlikely that these activities took place on Babbacombe Beach itself, as the Coastguard Station was situated there; anyone wading ashore with contraband would have been easily spotted. However, there were several suitable places nearby, including Ansteys Cove which was named after a famous smuggler. Customs officers were apprehending drug traffickers there over a century later.

Blood was found inside the sleeves of Lee's great-coat, suggesting he had been out on the night of the murder. Did Emma Keyse hear him come back that night with someone and descend the stairs to investigate his activities and die for her trouble, leaving Lee to take the blame for one of his accomplices?

Many years later the *Western Morning News* reported that smugglers were active in the area at the time: *'Just before the crime - 94 casks of brandy had been apprehended, each cask containing between four and five gallons.'*

THE BUILDER

In February 1985, the *Exeter Weekly News* published the account of Mr Ken Goss, who revealed that his grandfather had told him in 1937 what had occurred on the night of the murder, and sworn him not to repeat what he knew until 100 years after the attempted hanging.

The murderer was a wealthy, well-respected local builder who was acquainted with Miss Keyse. According to Mr Goss's grandfather, Lee met the killer on the stairs, but was blackmailed into taking the blame as the builder knew that Lee had got a certain young lady 'into trouble'. The builder then bribed the prison carpenter to rig the gallows. What the builder's motive was is not explained. However the builder was only one of a number of neighbours and acquaintances of Miss Keyse who became the subject of local gossip. One week after the murder the *Torquay Directory* reported:

It has been summised that more than one person was concerned if not in the tragedy itself at least in its preparation and arrangement. There have been various rumours afloat on this point and even persons have been named without any warrant whatsoever.

THE FISHERMAN

Although Emma Keyse has been portrayed as a kindly old lady, well respected by Torquay Society, she had incurred the wrath of local fishermen when she refused them permission to erect capstans for their boats on the beach outside her house. This led to a county court action which the fishermen won, but they were understandably bitter at the elderly spinster's high-handed attitude which had threatened their livelihood.

The Babbacombe fishermen may well have had thoughts of revenge and when one named William Stiggins was found dead in the cottage he had rented from Miss Keyse, stories abounded that he had been involved in the crime.

The obituary of solicitor Isidore Carter published in February 1936 revealed that a county court case had been contested on Miss Keyse's behalf which may have reopened old wounds:

A fact which is not generally known in connection with this case was that Miss Keyse was a client of Mr Carter, and the day before the murder he had fought and won a case for her in Plymouth respecting certain beach rights.

THE SILVER DEALER

Another gentlemen who came under suspicion was local antiques dealer George Tregaskis, later owner of Torquay's Gibbons Hotel. In 1935, he told the Torquay *Herald & Express* that he had arranged to visit Miss Keyse on the night of her death, to value various objects.

Mr Tregaskis considered himself fortunate that he had changed his mind at the last moment, for if he had been found in possession of *objets d'art* bought from Miss Keyse, he may have become a prime suspect. He did not escape suspicion altogether however, and it was rumoured that the dealer had been asked by the police to account for his movements on the night of the murder.

His role in the Babbacombe murder was highlighted in the 1988 play *The Man They Couldn't Hang* written by Westcountry playwright Jane Beeson. Many years earlier, research by prominent local historian John Pike had also revealed a story about an expert in silver.

In November 1962, Mr Pike told the Torquay *Herald Express* that an informant was convinced that the executioner had been 'got at':

It seems that on the night of the murder three or four men, including Lee, were entertaining women at The Glen, when Miss Keyse interrupted them.

Apparently one of the men at the party was a 'dealer' in silver and in a position to pay the hangman.

Mr Pike said that he did not think that Lee was totally innocent of the crime, but he thought that someone else could have struck the blow and paid Lee to 'carry the can', assuring him that he would not hang. This could have been the dealer.

GEORGE TREGASKIS

George Tregaskis was for many years a silver dealer and owned a shop in Victoria Parade, Torquay. A slump in the antiques trade however persuaded him to become a licensed victualler and he remained at the Gibbon's Hotel on Torquay Strand for thirty-two years before retiring in 1935. Three years later he died at the age of 81.

A notable personality in Torquay's business, social and sporting life, he often used to relate how he had made an appointment to see Miss Keyse who wanted to show him some antiques she wished to sell. At the last moment he decided to go to the theatre, and on the same evening she was murdered. Had that meeting taken place Tregaskis used to say, he might have been implicated in the crime.

A keen boxer in his youth, who gave lessons to the gentry, Tregaskis had a violent temper. He used to boast of how he had turned on a schoolmaster who was giving him a thrashing, causing the teacher to flee for his life. On another occasion he was arrested for beating a man senseless in the street. The 'rough' had passed a rude remark about the young lady Tregaskis was escorting. Fortunately the man recovered and an unrepentant Tregaskis was released without charge.

'You see,' he said, *'I was pretty well known, and although a fighter, I was never a bully, but if anyone insulted me and went about looking for trouble they usually got it.'*

THE LOVER

The father of Elizabeth Harris's child has been the subject of much conjecture, and it is generally believed that if John Lee was innocent, this transient figure becomes a prime suspect. It was tentatively suggested by defence counsel in his summing up at Lee's trial, that Harris's lover may have been responsible for the crime, but no attempt was made in cross-examination to elicit his name or account for his whereabouts on the night in question.

Lee left people close to him in no doubt that his half-sister could provide the answers to clear him. The Prison Chaplin, Reverend John Pitkin, quizzed Lee incessantly in the condemned cell asking him to confess to the crime or name the man responsible. Their conversations resulted in the following communication to the Home Secretary:

After pressing John Lee for the 50th time almost to tell me the name of the man whom he states as being at The Glen with his half-sister on the night of the murder of

---

Miss Keyse, he yesterday said he would not swear to him, but he believed him to be Cornelius Harrington, a Babbacombe Fisherman. His half-sister, he said, can give the man's name.

Cornelius Harrington was subsequently investigated and interviewed personally by the Chief Constable of Devon. He was found to be a thoroughly respectable person, had never been seen at The Glen, and was at home on the night of the murder. Elizabeth Harris also stuck to her story that she had gone to bed early feeling unwell and the first she knew of the tragedy was when she smelt smoke.

It was also widely reported at the time that Lee had also made a statement to the Vicar of Abbotskerswell, implicating two people. He claimed that he had been awoken on the fateful night by someone passing his bed, and had also seen a man on the premises wearing a mask.

By the time Lee was released from prison, he reverted to his original story that he had slept throughout the events. In his serialised newspaper story, he even gave an example of another murder that had occurred where people in close proximity had not heard anything while they slept. Publicly, this was the version he presented; privately, he was seeking evidence that would clear him, even though he had had an extraordinary reprieve from the death penalty, served his time and was now a celebrity.

He revealed his true thoughts to the Home Secretary:

Being a innocent man I hope before many weeks to get the confession of my step-sister Elizabeth Harris the cook who confessed to the crime on her death-bed to Major Pearson a Salvation Army Officer.

The Home Office could find no evidence to support stories of the 'cook's confession'. The Lee family had no contact with Elizabeth Harris after the murder case and evidently had no first-hand knowledge that she had died. There is in fact, no official record of her death occurring between the birth of her daughter in May 1885, and August 1887 when the newspaper reports of her death-bed confession appeared. It has been suggested that Lee was Elizabeth Harris's lover. She was not engaged to be married, nor was she 'walking out' with any young man, and as her baby was later born in the Workhouse there was evidently no support forthcoming from the child's father.

Lee set fire to the house in order to kill Elizabeth and obliterate all traces of his incestuous relationship, killing his employer when she descended the stairs to investigate the smell of smoke.

This theory would explain why Elizabeth was only too willing to give evidence for the prosecution, and why Lee tried to deflect blame on to a lover he could not identify by making a statement that there had been a 'man in a mask' with his half-sister at the scene of the crime.

ELIZABETH HARRIS

Illegitimate daughter of John Lee's mother, Elizabeth Hamlyn Easterbrook Harris was born in Torbryan on 20 August 1855 and raised by her maternal grandmother, Bessie, whose second husband William Stevens owned Pepperdon Farm, Kingsteignton.

Prior to replacing her half-sister Millie as cook at The Glen in 1882, she worked in the service of Teignmouth bank manager Edward Chant.

Unmarried and expecting a child at the time of the crime, it was suggested by Lee's counsel that her lover might have killed Emma Keyse when discovered leaving The Glen.

Although at the trial she testified against Lee, she broke down in tears when the death sentence was passed. Her family later turned against her for giving evidence against her half-brother.

Her daughter Beatrice was born at Newton Abbot Workhouse on 24 May 1885. Elizabeth disappeared after the birth of her child and it was said that she had gone abroad.

It was widely reported in August 1887 that 'the cook' had admitted her part in the Babbacombe Murder on her death-bed. The 'confession' was emphatically denied by the Home Secretary, but Lee went to considerable lengths after his release trying to prove its existence.

On the morning of his execution, Lee wrote to his sister Millie:

'You must forgive Lizzie, I do forgive her - it is my fault I ought to have opened my mouth before.'

CHAPTER 10 A GRAVE INJUSTICE?

If we assume that Elizabeth's lover did have some connection with the murder of Miss Keyse we now have to look at who he might have been. There were many male visitors to The Glen, who may have been attracted to the young servant, including nobles and the gentry. The most common theory however, proposes that the killer was a prominent local man, confirmed in a story which appeared in the Torquay *Herald & Express* in March 1936, when a man 'known and respected by every citizen of Torquay' approached the paper with revelations that Lee had covered up for the real murderer of Emma Keyse.

The article revealed that a well known young man, highly respected and very popular, was buried in a South Devon town 'about the year 1890'. As the mourners dispersed, a man standing at the graveside remarked to his two sons, one of whom was the article's informant, ' We have buried this afternoon the secret of the Babbacombe murder.'

The two brothers did not fully understand the relevance of their father's comment until 1908, when John Lee sought their advice shortly after his release from prison. They were stunned to hear Lee's claim that the man whose funeral they had attended was the murderer. Lee explained that this man had been 'carrying on' with a young woman at The Glen. On the night of the murder the man had organised a late-night supper party in the kitchen of The Glen. He was joined by Lee and two young women. The party was going well when they were suddenly disturbed by Miss Keyse who was ' livid with rage'.

'High words' followed, Miss Keyse slapped the young man's face, then told Lee to summon the police. The man in question, afraid his public career would be ruined, struck down the old lady with a hatchet. Everyone was in a state of panic, but Lee kept his head and suggested that they should make it appear there had been a burglary. He soaked the house with paraffin and set fire to the place, believing all evidence of what had taken place would be destroyed. Lee concluded by saying that when the plan failed and he was arrested he stuck to his story that he had heard and seen nothing, and his defence was paid for by the man in question.

The author of the newspaper article, respected journalist Reg Cowill, was convinced of the credentials of his informant and the authenticity of his story, though names were withheld to protect descendants of the family. Far from providing a satisfactory conclusion to the case therefore, the world was left with another unsolved mystery, and the identity of the alleged murderer has baffled anyone with an interest in the case, ever since the story was published. The true identity of the young man described in the 1936 article can now be revealed. Reg Cowill's article continues:

The man concerned, and who was declared by Lee to be the murderer of Miss Keyse, was known, says our informant, to have been critically ill for a long time after the murder, though nobody at that time - or ever - associated him with the crime. As a matter of fact, he never really recovered, and gradually became demented. He died in a mentally unbalanced condition ... When in his madness, he shouted things which the doctors put down to his state of mind, there were one or two people - our informants' father was one - who knew what he was referring to, and what had driven him insane.

It is well known that prior to Lee's trial his solicitor became indisposed, having represented the accused at both the Inquest and the Magistrates' Hearing. His younger brother deputised at the trial to instruct the defence counsel.

What never emerged however was how seriously ill Lee's solicitor was, but the defendant was all too well aware of how crucial this development had been to his case. He regularly petitioned the Home Secretary during his imprisonment protesting his innocence and on 1 November 1887, he wrote:

I wish to bring before your notice that the Solicitor that my parents employed to look after my case, was between the coroner's inquest and the trial taken with a fit of insanity and all that I had told him about the case and all that he himself had prepared was of no use and just as the trial commenced his brother took the case into hand, but had nothing ready for my Counsel.

In fact, the solicitor, Reginald Gwynne Templer never recovered. He died at Holloways Sanatorium, St Anns Heath, Virginia Water, Surrey. The cause of death was 'general paralysis of the insane'. He was buried in 'a South Devon town' at Teignmouth Cemetry - 'about 1890' - actually, on 23 December 1886. Was R Gwynne Templer the man described in Colwill's article?

If Templer was guilty of the allegations made by Lee, there is little wonder that the balance of his mind was disturbed. Defending someone for a crime he himself had committed, facing prosecution witnesses recounting details of his horrendous crime, questioning the woman who was bearing his child: these factors must have placed an intolerable strain on his conscience.

Before working at 'The Glen', Elizabeth Harris had been employed in service at Teignmouth, Templer's home town.

It was also discovered, by the informant, that the money for Lee's defence was provided by the man in question. In his autobiography Lee said that the costs were £60, which, as he was earning 2 shillings a week at the time of the murder, was equivalent to twelve years' pay, and more than one year's earnings for the average manual labourer. It has always been a mystery therefore how Lee's family found the money. The editor of the *East & South Devon Advertiser* launched an appeal hoping to raise £50 for Lee, but received only £12.

It was announced after the Magistrates' Hearing that two lawyers were to be engaged on behalf of Lee at his trial. Following Templer's indisposition however, this did not transpire, and a circuit barrister was retained.

It is generally agreed that the circumstantial evidence against Lee would not in itself have gained a conviction if tried today, although the advances in forensic science would have clarified many issues concerning the blood found on the alleged murder weapons and Lee's clothing. With a well-prepared case, the defence of the day should have been capable of gaining an acquittal. The loss of Gwynne Templer was crucial to Lee's trial, and the *East & South Devon Advertiser* expressed disquiet about these aspects of the case:

We heard the evidence that was given at the inquest, before the magistrates, and at his final trial at the Assizes, and we cannot but believe ourselves it was his cruel hand which committed the dreadful act. Still, whilst we believe this, we are bound in common

REGINALD GWYNNE TEMPLER

Reginald Gwynne Templer resided at Teignmouth, the eldest of six children born to Reginald William Templer and his wife Emily (née Gwynne). His father was the nephew of George Templer who until 1829 owned the 80,000 acre estate of Stover, near Newton Abbot. The family mansion is now an independent girls' school. George Templer was responsible for the construction of the now defunct Haytor Granite Tramway, and his father had been responsible for the creation of the Stover Canal (both now a Heritage Trail, the Templer Way), to carry granite from the Templer quarries on Dartmoor to the docks at Teignmouth. Ironically the business provided the stone for the construction of London Bridge, and it was in a nearby public house that the last positive sighting of John Lee was reported.

The Templer family built a church at Teigngrace, a small village on the Stover estate, where R Gwynne Templer's grandfather was Rector for many years. Following the death of her first husband Thomas, Elizabeth Keyse married George Whitehead and the couple settled in Teigngrace where in 1823, seven year old Emma Keyse was baptised by the Reverend John Templer.

Elizabeth Whitehead took up residence at The Glen following the death of her second husband in 1831. By the time of the murder, the association between the Templers and the Whiteheads was not generally known, though the fact emerged later that R G Templer was a confidante of Emma Keyse and a welcome visitor at her home. It is therefore surprising that he should come forward to defend Lee when he was so well acquainted with the victim.

Educated at Blundells public school in Tiverton, Templer was a prosperous eligible bachelor, and a member of a distinguished family who had lived in Devon since one of their ancestors landed at Brixham with William of Orange in 1688. In the class-conscious Victorian age, a dalliance between a gentleman and a female servant was deemed acceptable if conducted discreetly, though rarely resulting in marriage. Even the scandal of pregnancy would have not persuaded someone from Templer's background to jeopardise his social position by contemplating a match to a girl such as Elizabeth Harris.

justice to say there is room for some doubt. And we do not hesitate to assert that doubt might have been greatly strengthened in our minds, as well as in that of others, if the prisoner in the outset could have commanded money, in like manner as the prosecution did in netting around him strong evidence of guilt. Very rightly the prosecution spared no expense, not a stone was left unturned in fact, to produce even the most trifling bit of evidence against him. The prisoner on the other hand, had no such facilities. Shut up in the cells at Torquay he was debarred even an interview with his father, and though he was afterwards defended by a solicitor, that gentlemen falling ill, and remaining so up to the time of the trial, he was unable to render the counsel (Mr St Aubyn) who represented the prisoner at the Assizes but comparatively little assistance. The loss sustained in this respect must have been all the more severely felt when two eminent counsel were engaged for the prosecution. Not only was the evidence against the prisoner very strong, but it was systematically linked together in the absence of any material cross-examination to snap or weaken any of these links that the jury had no other alternative but to return the verdict which they did. Had Mr St Aubyn been more fully instructed it is possible that many more important facts might have been elicited in cross-examination in the prisoner's behalf.

THE INFORMANT

Reg Cowill's article explained how John Lee sought advice from two brothers who had attended the funeral of the guilty party with their father. Isidore Carter had died just before the revelations were published, therefore it has been assumed that he was the father of Cowill's unnamed informant. Although Carter had two sons, he was divorced by their mother in 1885 for adultery and desertion. He lived with his mistress near Teignmouth, in the neighbouring village of Shaldon, but a year after such a scandal, he was in no position to take his sons to the funeral of a professional acquaintance. R G Templer's two brothers can also be ruled out as Cowill's informant, for the article stated that Lee had no idea that the people he visited knew the dead man.

Two brothers who were approached by Lee in 1908 were Teignmouth solicitors Hutchings & Hutchings, who wrote to the Home Office on his behalf, seeking permission for Lee to relate his experience on the scaffold to religious societies. Their father was Thomas Hutchings, the first Chairman of Teignmouth Urban District Council, also a solicitor, and a contemporary of Templer's father at the time of the funeral.

The younger of the two brothers, Ernest Hutchings, became a leading citizen of Torquay. He was dubbed 'the stranger from Teignmouth' by his political opponents when elected onto the town council in 1901. Advocating the provision of many leisure and sporting facilities, he did much to develop Torquay as a holiday resort. After declining offers to become Mayor of Torquay and Parliamentary candidate for the Liberal Party, he was appointed Devon County Coroner. Cowill described his source as a man 'known and respected by every citizen of Torquay' which is a fitting tribute to the work of Ernest Hutchings. His interest in the case of John Lee may be explained by an illuminating comment about his life and career made in the *Torquay Directory* which described him as 'a man with a passion for justice'.

Why Lee chose to shield Templer is at first sight not wholly clear. Lee may have had little concern at the fate of Templer and Harris but, as the law stood at the time, all witnesses to the crime were considered accessories before the fact and liable to be charged with murder. According to the informant's story, there was a fourth person in the kitchen of The Glen on the night of the murder, a young woman; if the lady concerned was Lee's fiancée Kate Farmer, then Lee would have had every incentive to protect her and take the consequences.

Kate attended Lee's committal still wearing her engagement ring, which the police had returned after establishing it had not been taken from the murdered lady. Lee wrote a letter to his sweetheart on the eve of his execution, which was withheld by the prison authorities who interpreted a reference he made saying that he deserved hanging for being so foolish as 'to let things go', tantamount to a confession.

The couple had no further contact, and eighteen months after the murder Kate married a Plymouth seaman, James Parrish, who had himself been involved in a murder trial, having overpowered a shipboard assasin. They settled in Westhill, Torquay, until April 1891, when coincidentally, on the same day that former Glen servant, Jane Neck was buried, James Parrish found a note from his wife saying she was leaving and would never return.

Soon after Lee's release, the press located Kate in Plymouth, where she was living with her twenty-one year old daughter. She ruled out any hope of a romantic reunion with her former sweetheart, saying,

He has suffered. I hope his future life will be happy . . . I hope he may be able to prove his innocence . . . I remember most vividly the last time I saw him. It was at the inquest. I recall he walked with his head in the air, although he was in deadly peril. He recognised me and smiled, and said, 'Goodbye my dear.' Those were the last words I heard him utter. He never sent a letter from prison to me, and he never asked me to visit him in Portland. My friends told me that Lee would be kept in prison as long as he lived, and a life's devotion would be thrown away. So I put him out of my heart.

Was John Lee guilty? Did he relate a true account of events to the unnamed informant and his brother in 1908? Reg Colwill was certain of one thing as he concluded his article:

. . . there is no question whatever that the statements referred to in this article were made by Lee and the other persons mentioned and if Lee spoke the truth - and the other events seem to prove that there was more than 'something' in what he said - it looks as though after all this time the world has come to know what really happened in The Glen on that night in November over fifty years ago.

If Lee's story *is* to be believed, then after a further period of over fifty years, the world can now share the secret of the Babbacombe Murder.

FURTHER READING

The following books and extracts relating to the author's research are available in the Local Studies Collection at Torquay Central Library :

HISTORICAL BACKGROUND TO THE AREA OF SOUTH DEVON

Delderfield, E R - *Torbay Story* (Raleigh 1951)
Ellis, A C - *An Historical Survey of Torquay* (Author 1930)
Harris, Helen - *The Haytor Granite Tramway and Stover Canal* (Peninsula Press 1994)
Pateman, Leslie Lownds (ed) - *Pictorial and Historical Survey of Babbacombe and St Marychurch*
    (Babbacombe & St Marychurch Traders and Hoteliers Association 1980)
Snell, F A - *Devonshire* (W. Mate Ltd. 1907)
White, J T - *History of Torquay* (Author 1878)

ACCOUNTS OF THE PARTICIPANTS AT THE ATTEMPTED EXECUTION OF JOHN LEE

Lee, John - *The Man They Could Not Hang* (Mellifont Press 1908, Devon Books 1988, Musikfolk 1992)
Berry, James - *My Experiences as an Executioner* (Percy Lund & Co. 1892)
Pitkin, Reverend John - *The Prison Cell in its Light and Shadows* (Samson, Low, Marton & Co. 1918)

BOOKLETS ON THE BABBACOMBE MURDER PUBLISHED BY AUTHORS

Keyse, Frank - *The Babbacombe Murder* (1988) - author descendent of the victim
Croker, Paul - *John Babbacombe Lee* (1980) - student design project

EXTRACTS ON JOHN LEE AND THE BABBACOMBE MURDER

Atholl, Justin - *The Reluctant Hangman* (Long 1956)
Bland, James - *Crime Strange But True* (Warner Books 1991)
Brown, Theo - *Devon Ghosts* (Jarrolds 1982)
Halifax, Lord - *Lord Halifax's Ghost Book* (Geoffrey Bles Ltd. 1936)
Harrison, Peter - *Devon Murders* (Countryside Books 1992)
Honeycombe, Gordon - *More Murders of the Black Museum* (Hutchinson 1993)
Lauder, Rosemary Anne & Williams, Michael - *Strange Stories of Devon* (Bossiney 1982)
Lawrence, John - *Seaside Crimes* (c 1920 publisher unknown)
Logan, Guy BH - *Rope, Knife & Chair* (Stanley Paul 1928)
Pateman, Leslie Lownds (ed) - *Pictorial and Historical Survey of Babbacombe and*
    St Marychurch, Vol. 2 (Babbacombe & St Marychurch Traders and Hoteliers Association 1991)
Pike, Andrew & Cooper, Ross - *Australian Film 1900 - 1977* (Oxford University Press in
    association with The Australian Film Institute, Melbourne 1980)
Singer, Kurt (ed) - *Tales From the Unknown* (WH Allen 1970)
Walbrook, H M - *Murders and Murder Trials 1812 - 1912* (Constable 1932)
Wilson, Colin (ed) - *Murder in the Westcountry* (Bossiney 1975)
Yeats-Brown, F (ed) - *Escape* (c 1950 publisher unknown)

SOURCES OF INFORMATION

The author wishes to express his grateful thanks for the information provided by the staff of the following departments:

RECORD OFFICES

Public Record Office, Kew, Surrey · Greater London Record Office · Devon Record Office, Exeter

REGISTER OF BIRTHS, MARRIAGES & DEATHS

General Register Office - St Catherine's House, London · Family History Centre - Church of Latter Day Saints, Plymouth · Cornwall Local Studies Library - Redruth · Newton Abbot Register Office

LOCAL STUDIES LIBRARIES IN THE FOLLOWING CITIES AND TOWNS

Blackburn · Bradford · Bristol · Exeter - Westcountry Studies Library · Leeds · London - Guildhall Library, Marylebone Library, Southwark Local Studies Library, Westminster City Archives · Manchester Middleton · Nelson · Newcastle-upon-Tyne · Plymouth - Naval History & Local Studies Library · Torquay · York

OVERSEAS LIBRARIES

New York Public Library - USA · Toronto Public Library - Canada · State Library of New South Wales - Sydney, Australia

PROBATE REGISTRY OFFICES

Principal Registry - Somerset House, London · Probate sub-registry - Eastgate House, Exeter · Probate sub-registry - Market St, Bodmin